Maintaining Momentum in Long- Range Planning

Maintaining Momentum in Long-Range Planning

Merritt L. Kastens

amacom

American Management Associations

This book is available at a special
discount when ordered in bulk quantities.
For information, contact Special Sales Department,
AMACOM, a division of American Management Associations,
135 West 50th Street, New York, NY 10020

Library of Congress Cataloging in Publication Data

Kastens, Merritt L.
    Maintaining momentum in long-range planning.

    Companion vol. to: Long-range planning for your business. c1976.
    Includes index.
    1. Corporate planning. I. Kastens, Merritt L.
Long-range planning for your business. II. Title.
HD30.28.K37   1984   658.4'012   84-45205
ISBN 0-8144-5789-4

Printing number

10 9 8 7 6 5 4 3 2 1

*To **Anita***
who suffers when I am
working on a book.

Preface

"I never promised you a rose garden." My previous book *Long-Range Planning for Your Business* (New York: AMACOM, 1976) promised an operating manual for a simple business planning cycle. I never said it would be easy. Golf is a simple game. For most people it is far from easy.

This book is written for managers who have had four or five years of experience with long-range planning—managers who have had firsthand experience with the benefits it can bring and with the stumbles and hang-ups to which all planning processes are heir. It is a sequel to, not a revision of, the earlier book, so it will not repeat any of the basic techniques previously described. You are cordially invited to get a copy of the first book if you want to start from scratch.

Emphasis again is on the operational aspects of the planning process—upon what you *do* rather than on concepts and constructs. Since you should now be beginning to feel somewhat at ease in the planning mode, we will consider some appropriate embellishments of your process—ways in which you can make it both more comprehensive and at the same time more precise.

We will also deal with correctives for some of the problems that commonly afflict planning procedures after the first few planning cycles, when the initial enthusiasm has begun to wane and the easy familiarity with the techniques has not been quite yet attained. In fact, if this book seems unduly therapeutic, it is simply because of the prevalence of a kind of sophomore slump commonly experienced a few years after the initial introduction of formal planning. In its most pernicious form, the loss of momentum arises because the process has gotten mired in a lot of forms and formalities that are being fulfilled mechanically with neither credibility nor accountability. These cases often require rather heroic measures to get back to basics and to design a new "plan for planning." The first principle of planning has been violated. Focus on the results—the objective. The objective of planning is to gain control over the future direction of the enterprise, not to fill a lot of spread sheets and notebooks. "Having lost sight of our objectives, we redoubled our efforts." Don't do it! It won't work.

More likely, though, frustration arises from a growing awareness that the planning is not coming to grips with the "really important issues." What that probably means is that the planning itself has spotlighted the really important issues and will not let you sweep them under the carpet. That is what planning is supposed to do, and there are systematic ways to seek the solutions. The planning process will not give you the answers, but it will help you look for them. I will suggest some ways to look.

A lot of things have happened since the first book was written—most of them bad. The impressive thing about the recent tough times has been the spread in the performance among companies that were nominally in the same business. Some companies actually came through with growth and profits virtually unimpaired, while others in the same industry were filing under Chapter 11 or worse. Even in the most depressed industries, some people at least kept their footing while others floundered. It is undoubtedly true that "a rising tide raises all boats." It is equally true, though not as often remarked, that in a falling tide the boats that are anchored in shoal water go aground while others still have ample water under their keel.

Management does make a difference. Some executives actually earn the big salaries that they draw. The ones who do invariably have a well-thought-out notion of where they want to go and a system to assure that the important things get done and the irrelevant things get stopped. They have a strategy and a control system. They have a plan. We will talk a good deal about strategy and control.

Now we have said that word—*strategy*. The earlier book very consciously and explicitly avoided the term. It avoided the term for the simple reason that it frightened a lot of people and it seemed preferable to stick to the straightforward discussion of objectives and actions and not get mixed up with anything quite so elegant. However, in the intervening years *strategy* has been so omnipresent in the management literature, and so many strange and wonderful things have been proposed in its name, that we have to say something about it.

Strategy is a good thing. We should have more of it—lots more! It boils down to being "in the right place at the right time." That cliché has been around for a long time. The trouble is few people knew how to find the right place at any particular time. It was mostly a matter of luck.

Luck will not do it anymore. There are too many bright strategists out there looking for that right place—that "niche" is what they usually call it. Let's face it. A plan is always *against* something. A plan is *right*, compared to what? Compared to the nature of the opportunity. Compared to what the competition is doing—or will do. Compared, for that matter, to what the government will do. We will give more attention this time around to finding out just what it is that you are planning against, not that this was not always important, but because you should now be able to handle more dimensions of input than you could when you were just starting.

We will talk a little more about people, too. The recent rough patch weeded out some of the real clinkers, but the people who survived did not panic as much as they were expected to. People are getting harder to live with. You cannot move them around so easily. They have notions about the kind of life-style they want. They even expect satisfaction from their work. You have to plan for that, too.

As before, the book is written as if addressed to a chief executive officer. This is a stylistic device to present a consistent point of view. The text is actually intended for anyone who has decision-making and resource-allocating responsibilities—the "unit presidents" if you will. Every manager is a CEO on his or her own turf.

The chapters in this book correspond in content pretty much to chapters from *Long-Range Planning for Your Business*. They are of unequal length because some subjects seem to warrant more elaboration than others. Chapters 1 through 3 correspond. Chapter 4 from my earlier book corresponds to Chapters 4 and 5 of this book. (This is an important topic, and the chapter got too long!) As a result, Chapter 5 from *Long-Range Planning for Your Business* correlates with Chapter 6 of this book, and Chapter 6 from the previous book correlates with Chapter 7 of this one. With Chapter 8 the correlation breaks apart, but the message is there in a different format.

The units of the planning process have been rearranged somewhat and in some cases combined. The earlier book showed the process in something like an "exploded" engineering drawing. The process was presented in small bites that could be viewed, grasped, and implemented one at a time. More experienced planners should be able to encompass larger units of input at a single sitting. It is also assumed that the quality of preparation will be better, so that it is not necessary to provide as much opportunity for recycling. I am also assuming that a planning team of more or less fixed composition has been established, since this has become almost universal practice. With these factors in mind, I've revised the annual planning schedule that appeared as Figure 2 in the earlier book. The new version is Figure 1 in the first chapter of this book.

As in the earlier book, cleaning up the grammar and straightening out the syntax were done by Anita S. Kastens and the typing and retyping by Audrey J. Snyder. These two super ladies are just as good as ever. Jan Moreland joined the team this time around.

For Additional Information

Kastens, M. L., *Long-Range Planning for Your Business: An Operating Manual* (New York: AMACOM, 1976).

If you haven't read this, you should. It will make this book easier to follow!

Thurston, P. H., "Should Smaller Companies Make Formal Plans?" *Harvard Business Review*, Vol. 61, No. 5 (September–October 1983), pp. 162–184.

Nothing particularly new, but good sound stuff well expressed in practicable terms and directed explicitly at the small company.

Contents

1
Change—Action—
Accountability

There is nothing more difficult of success, nor more dangerous to handle, than to initiate a new order of things.

—NICCOLO MACHIAVELLI

The objective of all planning is to gain control of your own destiny and that of your organization: to make the outfit go where you point it. If it still feels like you are riding on a roller coaster or if there is too much play in the tiller, you are not doing it right. You are not getting full value for the time and effort expended. All the forms and models, the meetings and reports are means to an end. If they do not produce a positive linkage to direction of progress, they are not worth the time.

This is not to say you can aspire to control all aspects of a business. It would be naive to expect to. You want to control those things that are controllable and be assured of a quick and constructive response to the external events that are not controllable. You cannot control the incidence of potholes in the highway, but sometimes you can avoid the rough stretches. And when you do hit a spring buster, you want a vehicle that will not get thrown off the road—particularly if you are traveling at high speed. If your steering mechanism is not performing up to expectations, maybe it needs new stabilizer rods or maybe we can tighten up the linkage.

A road map helps. The typical planning schedule shown in Figure 1 is a more sophisticated version of the planning schedule in the earlier book. With some planning experience behind you, you should be ready to work within such a framework.

Change

The first place to look is at the basics. Change is the essence of planning. You plan for change. You do not need a formal plan to tell people to keep doing what they have always done. People do not like to change. It is uncomfortable. It may be dangerous. If you have had a planning process for several years, you know this only too well. You probably know who the problem individuals are.

How many times have I been asked, "How do you make people think strategically?" If I knew, I would bottle the formula and sell it. You can lead them up to the trough and stick their noses in the water, but if all they will do is snort and kick, maybe you had better get new horses.

There are some tricks, however, and one of them is central to the planning mentality, although it is frequently forgotten. The one intellectual innovation of the whole planning concept is that it involves ends-to-means logic. This is where planning gets its power—that is, how it encourages and even forces original thinking. Conventionally, the responsible manager has tried to anticipate the consequences of his or her potential action. "What might be the consequences if I took such and such an action?" The planned manager says, "If I want to achieve such and such an objective, how might I possibly get there?" Ends first, then means. It is a big difference.

To make planning work, you have to clamp down really hard on extrapolative-type thinking—on the kind of thinking people habitually do in making out a budget. "If we did this a little better and that a little more, we should be able to make

Figure 1. Revised version of a typical planning schedule.

	Jan.	Feb.	Mar.	Apr.	May	June	July	Aug.	Sept.	Oct.	Nov.	Dec.
Market analysis	■											
Strategy meeting		■										
Planning review												
Mission												
Policies												
Environmental review			■									
Markets												
Competition												
General												
Key result objectives												
Action plans			■	■								
Threats and opportunities				■	■							
SBU planning				■	■	■	■					
Development planning					■	■	■	■				
Administrative plan				■								
Corporate operations analysis												
Trends												
Strengths				■	■							
Weaknesses												
Action plans												
Strengths												
Weaknesses					■							
Corporate plan I						■						
Facilities plan							■	■				
Financial plan												
Corporate plan II									■			
Budget										■		

so much." That might get you incremental gains, but it seldom leads to real change. You must force your people to set their objectives first. "With our competitive advantages, we ought to be able to grow substantially faster than the total market," or "We have to get at least a 10 percent share of market in order to be competitive." Then challenge your people to come up with ideas to make it happen. It won't always work, but it is certainly worth a try. Technically, this is a planning gap analysis. You can do it with varying degrees of formality, and we will consider some of the techniques in more detail later. But the principle is to force people to dredge up some new and different ideas.

The big hazard is that you will get a lot of blue sky: wishful thinking. Maybe you have found that out already. The antidote is to put more rigor into your review and approval procedure. Stated bluntly, you must set up an adversary procedure or, if you prefer, a selling situation. Make people convince you that their ideas are sound.

Practice Makes Perfect

The first step is to refuse to spend time on half-thought-out ideas. If someone wants to recommend a program, insist that the available facts be assembled and organized and that the program steps be laid out in detail with costs, times, and probabilities specified. If the proposal is not complete, refuse to let anyone spend any time considering it. Send the author back to the drawing board to get his or her stuff together no matter how intriguing the idea is. If nothing else, this will save a lot of executive time. The practice is extremely valuable if you have a planning committee. I warn you: It will not work the first time. But if you keep ushering people out of your office with some sympathetic encouragement and a promise of serious consideration when "everything is ready," eventually even the most obtuse individual will get the message.

You must insist that people do their homework and come up with a complete package. In the first place, as noted above, it saves everybody's time. It also permits you to simplify your planning routine while at the same time enabling you to get more people involved in the detailed decision making. It will enable you to use a more sophisticated planning schedule and take it in bigger and more comprehensive bites.

Another important reason to insist on adequate staff work is to get information inputs that are in sufficient detail and with a level of reliability that will permit you to compare and relate elements of the plan within a coherent whole. One of the reasons that you have a formal planning process is so that you can consider the entire array of options at one time. If you consider programs individually, you run the risk of suboptimization. Each of the programs may look attractive by itself, but if you add them all up, they do not make sense. They may be contradictory or at least not intersupportive. Individually they may be fine. Collectively they may be impossible.

A common experience of organizations first beginning to plan is that they get overcommitted. The very nature of the process will bring up so many opportunities—and problems—that they cannot all be handled at once. Some will have to be deferred, stretched out, dropped. The problem is not so often a shortage of money; it is the limits of people's time. Your planning process must provide an opportunity to draw up a resource budget to assure that your plans are realistically doable. Otherwise planning can get you into trouble. By and large, people do not muff an assignment or do a half-assed job through ignorance, incompetence, or irresponsibility. People, particularly the good ones, unwittingly commit themselves to more than is humanly possible to accomplish. This kind of overcommitment deludes the organization into false expectations and leads to feelings of guilt and low morale in the individual. Nobody wins.

You guard against overcommitment in two primary ways. Insist that people think through their programs thoroughly before accepting responsibility for their fulfillment. And have a planning process that permits each individual to see at one time the totality of the responsibilities he or she is being asked to accept for some reasonable period into the future. Guard yourself against the "willing horse" who reflexively says "Sure, boss, we can do that." Your response to that should be, "What are you going to stop doing—or have you been sitting around on your hands with a lot of idle time?"

But to do all this, you need coherent input units to work with, not a box of assorted bits and pieces that might or might not be assembled into a working machine. You need numbers you can add, time scales you can measure. Reasonable estimates. You do not need great precision, just enough to permit a logical decision about whether the pieces might fit together.

In the real world, it is very difficult, if not impossible, to get all your program proposals together for one deadline in order to do the kind of resource budget referred to above. One piece of input information is going to be missing. Something will come up in the middle of a planning cycle. But you can work toward the ideal. Use rough estimates when you must, and label them as such. Then upgrade them when you have the hard facts. That is one of the virtues of a formal plan. It is easy to modify and recalculate a well-structured plan. If everything is extemporaneous, it is hard to change because you never know what you are changing.

In the real world, also, it is going to be hard to get all this staff work done if your people are not used to doing it. Since we are committed to the principle that the people who are going to be in charge of implementation are the ones who must make the plans, you are going to have a lot of doers involved in thinking through their actions, and they are likely to resist. The only prescription is: "Practice makes perfect." Be patient but insistent, and demand that they keep doing the task until they get it right. It will come—in most cases.

Action

If you create a situation in which people are forced to come up with suggestions for change and you decide which innovations are the right innovations, you still must see that something is done about it. Everything in a planning procedure should be aimed at an ultimate action. Otherwise you end up with a kind of scenario that may or may not ever get on the stage. Eventually, you must get to the point where you put down in writing who is going to do what, when, and with which.

This may sound a little obvious, but a remarkable number of organizations seem to run out of steam when they get to this final planning step. It is kind of slogging work. The inspired thinking and the decision making has all been done. But the detailing must be done for two reasons. It is the only responsible way to confirm the cost/benefit numbers. And it focuses responsibility down to individuals.

Certainly action planning is a detailed procedure, but it is also an attitude that should pervade the entire planning process. If you are setting policies, they should be stated in terms that will mandate or prohibit certain types of actions. If you make an assumption about an environmental factor, ask immediately, "What should we do about it?" If you claim a strategic strength, decide then and there how it could be exploited in ways it is not now being used.

Get the habit. Make it a reflex. No planning is meaningful unless it is actionable. Otherwise it is merely an intellectual exercise.

Accountability

There is one other principle that is central to successful planning. Planning must be done in a culture of strict accountability. Anyone who accepts responsibility for a strategic program must truly expect to achieve the stated objective. The responsible individual is probably the author of the program, but even if this is not the case, once the assignment is acknowledged, it must be accepted in dead earnest. If there are any reservations, you want them to come out before the action is undertaken—not when the expected results are not forthcoming.

If you deviate from this principle, your plans are likely to be no more than a wish list. As George Dively, late president of Harris Intertype, used to say, "If you accept excuses, you will get excuses." They will be plausible excuses, but you cannot put them in the bank.

Which is not to say that every plan is going to be perfect.

There are going to be some out-and-out bummers. But when a program begins to go badly off the track, the person in charge should be clearly aware of the collateral responsibility to come in and insist that the objective be changed. As long as the program leader is confident that the original objectives can be achieved, he or she can be allowed great flexibility in altering the specific action steps to achieve them. The program leader should inform his or her superior if an action program is changed but not necessarily seek prior approval. What you want is *constancy of purpose and flexibility in action.* But you can only achieve that flexibility—you can only allow that flexibility—if the purpose is clearly and uniformly understood and there is an individual who acknowledges personal accountability for its attainment. If the responsible person wants to renegotiate that accountability, that's what you want to know about, and you want to know about it as early as possible.

In a well-structured plan, you must be able to depend on all the pieces being available when needed because you presumably have fully committed all the resources available. If one of the pieces is not going to work, you may be able to redesign the structure if you are aware of the problem in time. If you get to the final assembly and the piece is missing, you may have the equivalent of 95 percent of an automobile, but one that won't run. You have to be able to count on the results performance of your people or on a very early warning that the original planning judgment was flawed and a redesign is necessary.

So there you have the essential elements of successful planning: The need for change must be acknowledged; a mechanism leading to purposeful action must be built in; and strict accountability must be accepted.

You notice that the essential elements are basically matters of attitude, not procedure. But the attitudes, the organizational culture, must be friendly, or planning will not work. There is a kind of inherent rejection mechanism that will slough off the incompatible tissue if you try to graft a rational, planned management style onto a shoot-from-the-hip management body. Attitudes can be changed, but it is a tricky operation. One of the safest ways to do it is through what has come to be called "behavior modification." Change what people do, and let it feed back into the way they think. So let's talk about what people do when they go about planning.

For Additional Information

Allen, L. A., *Making Managerial Planning More Effective*. New York: McGraw-Hill Book Company, 1982.

One of the very few other writers on planning who emphasizes the essentiality of individual accountability. See Chapter 4: ". . . plans become useful tools and not display pieces only to the extent we can hold individuals accountable. . . . Theories of group or team accountability do not hold up in practice."

Cohen, S. M., "For GE, Planning Crowned with Success," *Planning Review* (March 1982), pp. 8–11.

Always a pioneer in planning, GE pushes ahead. Interesting concepts in control: "If [a manager] makes his budget at the expense of his strategy, he can be penalized for it. . . . No bonus!" The company watches for underspending as well as for overspending. "The new buzzword here is contention management." That is the intentional adversarial situation I am talking about.

Irwin, P. H., "Changing Organizational Behaviour through Strategic Planning," *Managerial Planning* (September–October 1979), pp. 3–5, 12.

Just what the title says it is.

Kastens, M. L., "Cogito, Ergo Sum," *Interfaces* (May 1972).

A little essay that has been reprinted in a number of places. If you can get ahold of a copy, read it. The message is: Management is a rational, "thinking" process.

Kastens, M. L., "The Why and the How of Planning," *Managerial Planning* (July–August 1979), pp. 33–35.

More on planning for change and what the plan document is and is not.

Peters, T. J., "Putting Excellence into Management," *Business Week* (July 21, 1980), pp. 196–205.

An early report on the findings of the McKinsey study on which the book In Search of Excellence: Lessons from America's Best-Run Companies *(Peters, T. J., and Waterman, R. H., Jr., New York: Harper & Row, 1982) is based. Well-run companies have a "bias toward action," use task forces to do things, not study them. Refers to Procter & Gamble's one-page memo rule.*

Tregoe, B. B., and Zimmerman, J. W., *Top Management Strategy*. New York: Simon & Schuster, 1980.

Tregoe is a behavioral scientist who has been thinking about decision-making processes for over 25 years. He has some cogent comments on how to encourage strategic thinking, particularly in Chapter 6, but it is a short book, so read it all. Unfortunately, there is a typical nomenclature problem. He defines "strategy formulation" and "long-range planning" as two different functions. "Strategic planning" as dealt with in this book corresponds pretty much to his concept of strategizing.

"When Strategic Planning Pays Off," *Chemical Week* (August 5, 1981), pp. 30–32.

A corporate-wide, comprehensive strategic planning system made it possible for DuPont to sit down with Conoco and in less than a week thrash out a tentative merger agreement. Without a plan, it could have taken months of preparation.

2
Don't Lose Your Concentration

Every enterprise needs a concept of its industry. There is a logical way of doing business in accordance with the facts and circumstances of an industry if you can figure it out.

—ALFRED P. SLOAN

If you have been planning for five years, you are due for major maintenance on your corporate mission statement. First, some questions.

Is the mission statement in fact giving you a sense of direction? Does it help you decide among strategic alternatives? Probably not! If your management is like most, you fudged the mission statement when you wrote it. Somebody said, "We don't want to fence ourselves in," so you compromised and slipped in some weasel words, such as ". . . and related products" or ". . . other selected markets." Or you used some grandiose language, such as "transportation" or "communication" or "human welfare," and built in a back door that anything could slip through.

Well, in five years you should have learned something. The planning experience should have focused your attention on at

11

least some of the critical dimensions of your business. You should have more and better and more pertinent information about your own organization and about the world in which you compete. You may have had some opportunities to choose among alternative strategies. Just what is the heart of your business? Where do you really make your money? During 1980–1983, a lot of companies had to figure this one out the hard way. The pruning and chopping was often quite severe. Chain retailers pulled out of whole sections of the country. So did gasoline retailers. Nationals became regionals. A lot of semiconglomerates dropped off noncoherent appendages. Sometimes they were fairly recently acquired divisions, but in some cases, the divestitures were old-time segments of the business that had lost their pertinence to the current thrust of the enterprise. Union Carbide got out of most of the ferroalloy business, which, as Electrometallurgical Company, had been part of the original merger that formed the corporation.

Concentration

The principle is focus, concentration. Professional athletes say that the minute you lose your concentration your opponent is going to score against you. Do what you do best where you can do it the easiest. The function of the mission statement is to define what and where that is. But *you* must do the definition.

Remember that a mission statement is not proscriptive. It defines the primary thrust of the enterprise, the area in which you will concentrate your best resources. It does not prohibit you from exploiting targets of opportunity or picking up business that comes your way along the margins. If you do not have the resources to be a power in the world market, the mission statement does not say you will not do some foreign business. It does remind you not to scatter your resources— including the president's time—all over the globe.

Setting the limits of the competitive arena for a company is probably the most important—and the most difficult— decision a manager is called upon to make. As competition becomes more skillful and more precisely focused, the selection of an optimum mission becomes ever more critical. Give it your best shot.

If you segment your business into strategic business units (SBUs), you will be faced with the same kind of decision on a smaller scale in determining the proper score for each SBU. More about that later.

Look at your mission statement critically. Can you tighten up the language to make the direction more explicit, to improve the focus? Can you prune out some meaningless or ambiguous words? Or is it time that you gave serious consideration to changing the nature of the business altogether? The successfulness of your plans in recent years may clue you to the answer to this last question.

Dumbbells and Siamese Twins

What if you decided your business is running down two parallel paths simultaneously with little likelihood that they will ever intersect? You have a dumbbell-shaped mission statement. Well, you might consider splitting the company in two. Seriously. If there is little or no connection between the two sides of the business, there is unlikely to be any significant synergism and they might both be better off on their own. That would at least save one layer of overhead. GAF Corporation came to this conclusion. So did Phillips Brothers. Very often the stock market looks favorably on such a separation. Financing may become easier for at least one of the former divisions. Recruiting of specialized talent may even be facilitated.

If you do not choose to perform this kind of corporate mitosis, you have two choices. You can plan for and manage the two divisions as if they were two separate companies, like Siamese twins connected at the treasurer's office. Or you can decide which one is your true love with which you want to spend the rest of eternity (corporations are immortal) and milk the other one until it shrivels into a vestigial appendix.

Corporations often find themselves in this situation when they break out of a dying industry and diversify into a completely different line of endeavor. This is an entirely proper course of action, but it's important to remember what you are doing and why you are doing it. Business units undergoing progressive abandonment have a pernicious way of hanging on to their deteriorating status long after reason or economics can justify their room and board. Nostalgia, an individual manager's mental comfort, and just plain inertia tend to provide refuge to the nominally rejected activity. It is not uncommon for operations to persist 20 years or more after the decision has been made to get out of the business. A straightforward statement of where the enterprise intends to go can sometimes stiffen the managerial backbone to the extent that managers will get on with the sometimes awkward task of redeploying resources out of the familiar patterns of the past and into the areas where the future will be made.

If you have more than two unrelated business thrusts, you are consciously or unconsciously on your way to becoming a conglomerate. If that is your intention, fine. You need a "resource manager" type of mission statement. You also need a different kind of organization structure and probably different kinds of managers.

Umbrellas

You may, of course, have several more or less discrete but related business segments that fit rationally within the overall concept of the corporation. In this case, you probably have a divisionalized corporate structure, with an umbrella mission for the corporation and individual missions or charters for each of the divisions. The question then arises as to whether the divisional charters must all be encompassed within the corporate mission. Probably not. You are better advised to keep the corporate thrust rather strictly focused, because otherwise you are apt to end up with a kind of a grab bag corporate statement that tries to make room for everybody. Rather, give your divisional managements a little scope to probe out beyond the strict limits of the parent's main business as long as they have a coherent concept of their own

strategic thrust. Just don't let them divert too many resources to these salients.

In a divisionalized company, a problem that is at least as
common is to find that, when you add up all the divisional
charters, they do not completely fulfill the corporate mission.
Again you have two choices: You can ask one or more of the
divisions to broaden their charters; you can set up a new
product or development department; or you can make an
acquisition. This may sound like three choices, but it's not
really. Internal development or acquisition are only two
alternative tactics for getting into a new line of business.
They involve a classical make-or-buy decision, although the
calculations may be a little more complex than trying to
decide whether to make or buy a product component.

Experience strongly suggests that the odds are best if you
set up a separate organizational entity—the second choice.
Directing a division manager to undertake an innovative
strategy that he or she did not personally devise is a little like
telling the research department to come up with a scientific
breakthrough by the end of the year. It is not very likely to
happen. Let the division manager run the business he or she
knows in the dimensions in which he or she conceives it, and
take on the responsibility at the corporate level to fill out the
gaps in the corporate mission.

The Corporate Strategy Meeting

Even if you have been formally reconsidering your corporate
mission every year, take a little extra time this year to step
back and look at the big picture. We said initially that you
should enlist "the people whose judgment you trust" to participate in this deliberation. This is still the right criterion.
However, by now you probably have established a formal or
de facto planning team. Close your office door, sit quietly for a
few minutes, and consider whether you have the right people
on the team. Planning teams have a tendency to grow and
become unwieldy. Sometimes they just start out too big.
Think back over the planning meetings of the past two years.
What people really made significant contributions? Were

there redundancies, two people who almost always made identical inputs? Do you need them both on the team? If your organization is divisionalized, what about the divisional general managers? Do they usually sit doodling until something comes up that affects their divisions? In large corporations, the divisional operating chiefs do not usually sit on the corporate strategic planning team. There is a simple reason for this: They would have split loyalties. They are supposed to concern themselves with the overall best interests of the corporation. But at the same time, they compete with the other divisions for the allocation of resources and often for their own personal bonuses. A certain parochialism is inevitable. In fact, it is desirable.

The same duality of interest can arise in a smaller company, and sometimes you have to live with it. There is just no other top management than the operating executives. Either the CEO makes all the planning decisions personally, or he or she invites the advice of the operating vice-presidents.

If, however, you feel that your planning team has gotten out of hand—is too big—there is a device to cut it down to size that is both defensible and functional. It is always difficult and frequently traumatic to ask someone who has participated in planning sessions in the past to step down from the team. But you can split the team in two—into a strategic planning group and an operational planning group. You can quite honestly plead economy in the use of time, particularly in a small organization.

Such a division may seem to violate the principle of having the planning decisions made by the people who will have to carry them out, and it will if it is not properly handled. It can create a we–they situation if objectives are set at the strategy level and imposed on the operating people. But if you retain the atmosphere of negotiated objectives, then nothing is fixed until it has been confirmed by all the appropriate levels of the hierarchy. There will be plenty for the operating people to do and ample opportunity for them to exercise their judgment and initiative.

To set the corporate mission, you need a team composed of only the people you want to determine the future destiny of the enterprise. If the group is not too large, you may want to augment it with an outside counsel, a consultant, or a board member who you feel can provide valuable perspective but who will not be involved in the more detailed planning decisions. But don't bring along any "tourists." Remember, if you double the size of the group, you have to quadruple the time you allow.*

When you have empanelled your strategy committee, take them off to a quiet place away from the office. Do it on a weekend if you must, but do not mix it up with a golf game or any other distractions—not even spouses. Take two days at a minimum. Two and a half days are better. It will take one day to back off from your day-to-day concerns and get a long-term perspective.

Planning Review

Use your first session to go back over your planning effectiveness for the past three to five years, not just last year's performance against plan. Some charts would be helpful. Concentrate on the key result objectives—sales, earnings, profitability, and the primary development objectives. Take them one at a time. Were you able to hold them pretty constant, or did you have to change them every year? If you had to change them, why? Write down on a chalkboard or easel pad all the reasons that made you feel you had to modify your objectives. Can you see any pattern in the reasons you have written? Did you repeatedly misjudge competitive actions? Were your new product objectives consistently over-optimistic? Were your cost projections misleading? Was your acquisition strategy a disaster? Did you fail to achieve the product mix the objectives called for? The answers to these kinds of questions will suggest changes in the upcoming planning cycle that will make it more successful:

*Mathematically, it is worse than that. Try calculating the sets of two you get out of a group of n members.

- Better market data.
- More thorough competitive analysis.
- Improved cost data and feedback
- Closer attention to the general environment.

Now take it a step further. For each one of your key objectives, even the ones you consistently achieved or exceeded, make two lists: one of the events that made it easier to reach the objective and the other of the events that made it significantly more difficult. Again, look for patterns. Are there some windfalls in there that you had not anticipated so that you really did not achieve the results you intended at all? Are there compensating errors that make the numbers come out all right but not really the way you planned? Is there some result area where you got all the bad breaks and still made the objective? Could be that somebody did a helluva good job and you should pay attention.

In 1977 you used an inflation rate of 6 percent per year in setting sales objectives. In the five years ending in 1982 the actual inflation rate was closer to 10 percent. If you set a sales growth objective of 15 percent per year based on a 6 percent inflation rate and your operating statements show an increase in sales revenue averaging 15 percent per year, you did not make your sales objective. You got a free ride from that extra 4 percent inflation and actually missed the objective by that much. On the other hand, a couple of years ago a lot of managements were counting on 8 and 10 percent inflation. With actual inflation around 5 or 6 percent, they might conclude that they were underperforming their objective when actually they were doing just fine.

You probably do not need to do this thorough a retrospective analysis every year, but you certainly should do it from time to time. You have to look at several years' performance to see significant patterns and trends. Annually, you should look at the previous year's performance against plan shortly after the year-end figures are available. That comparison, though, should be made at the first level of subobjectives below the key result objectives, because that is the corporate control level. It can be done somewhat later in the planning process.

Mission

With this view of the organization's strategic performance in recent years, you should be able to look at the corporate mission somewhat objectively. If you have been hitting your objectives regularly with very little strain, maybe you are not being sufficiently ambitious. Perhaps you should broaden the scope of the mission. Or if you fairly regularly did what you wanted to do with industrial products but did not make it with consumer products, maybe you just do not belong in the consumer market and should be honest with yourself. Or, now that you succeeded in getting your balance sheet in order and cleaned out some of the "dogs," perhaps you are ready to undertake a more aggressive mission. Or maybe your development objectives were consistently aborted because, even when you did the things you said you were going to do, you were quickly outgunned by the competition. You have to find a niche where you do not have to go toe-to-toe with these people. Or you might be positioned exactly right and should go full steam ahead. Obviously, you do not make these decisions casually; you should take time to thrash them out thoroughly!

A New Mission

What do you do if you have to face up to the fact that you are in an unfavorably structured industry? If you are big enough and bold enough, you can try to change the industry. Clorox did it in household bleach. Anyone with a few thousand dollars worth of equipment could cut and bottle sodium hypochlorite solution. But Clorox boosted the market ante, and the little guys could not follow. The same thing happened in potato chips, beer, and coffee.

Sometimes you can introduce new technology that cuts cost below even that of the garage operators but that is so capital intensive that it is not feasible for the smaller competitors. That is what happened in the automobile industry during the 1920s. It is happening now in food wholesaling with the introduction of automated warehouses. Iowa Beef

Packers (IBP) did it to beef packing, although the people IBP squeezed out were not so little. You might also say it is happening in American agriculture.

Of course, the ideal solution is to come up with a real innovation. Polyethylene resins were a pretty doggy business when Union Carbide researched and built, a substantially cheaper production process. There Carbide was, cozy as the Morton salt girl, under that big price umbrella provided by its competitors with their big expensive plants that they couldn't shut down, they couldn't scrap, and they couldn't sell. L'Eggs did it when they decided to market through supermarkets with a sharp point-of-purchase appeal. The trouble with that prescription, though, is: How do you whomp up a breakthrough, a real stroke of genius?

You can try to slide out from under the situation by staying in the industry but repositioning yourself into a more favorable role. Are either your suppliers or your customers substantially more profitable than you are? Can you move into their business, keeping your present operation as a supply source or captive market and making your money on the other step? This is what farmers think they are doing when they form a processing or distribution co-op. Sometimes it works. The quarry operator who goes into cement contracting or the scrap dealer who puts in an electric steel furnace is going this route. This vertical integration tactic is usually practical only if you are cash heavy, because either you have to make a lot of new investments or you have to make an acquisition. If you try to make an acquisition for stock, you are almost certain to come out on the short end of the price/earnings equation because you are trading a low–earnings-potential stock for one with higher potential.

A subtle twist on this maneuver is to sell out to your supplier. That company may not be able to survive without your business, and you can extract a favorable price. That is what the beet sugar people are trying to do in foisting off their sugar refineries on the beet growers. That is what happened when Visking sold out to Union Carbide.

Or you can change your mission. Redefine the industry. You are not in footwear; you are in fashion accessories. Take on belts and purses. You don't sell shoes; you sell glamour. Eventually, you may import your shoes. You are not a manufacturer of hand tools; you are a distributor of hardware items. Stanley tool did that! You do not run food stores; you are a merchandiser of household necessities. A lot of grocery chains are going this way—although some are taking off in the opposite direction, too.

You can define yourself right out of your industry—disassociate yourself from it. *Differentiation* is the popular term. If you have a unique product that is independent of the general trends in the market, that's great. Daimler-Benz, makers of Mercedes, did not behave like an automobile company at all in the early 1980s. They had superior engineering and sold to customers who didn't care about price, and the traumas that afflicted other auto producers passed right over them. Nice work if you can get it, but such situations seldom offer themselves through a simple act of will.

More practicable in most cases is a niche strategy. Find a segment of your industry market that does not suffer from the general lethargy of the industry—one that is growing faster, is less price sensitive, has special requirements—and concentrate your resources there. In a sense, that is what Mercedes does. A niche strategy means that you do not try to compete with the whole industry and usually means that you will settle for a smaller share of the total market. It also may mean that you can free up some resources to get into a more promising line of business.

The toughest tactic, as anyone in the military will tell you, is to effect a successful strategic retreat—get out of the business completely and at the same time build up something else. Peter Grace did it at W. R. Grace. Ben Heineman at Northwestern Railroad did it. And there are others. But there are a lot of corporate withdrawals that can only be compared to Napoleon's return from Moscow. If you decide you must do it, you will need the most careful kind of planning of all.

It is widely considered to be axiomatic that in a tight industry the key to survival is to be the low-cost producer. It is also generally agreed that it is foolish to put more investment into situations that promise only minimal returns. Unfortunately, these two dicta are sometimes contradictory. The decision ultimately becomes one of judgment and largely depends on how long you intend to tough it out. Short payback, cost-saving investments are usually justified. Long-term commitments to a situation with mediocre prospects at best, never are. You do not *have* to stay in the business. If worse comes to worst, you can always liquidate—and sometimes that can be an attractive alternative. If it is not attractive to the managers whose jobs might disappear, it could be attractive to a raider with no such personal position at stake.

Mission Accomplished

Before you leave the subject, be sure that you have solid concurrence among your top managers on the precise mission—the purpose, the grand strategy, the main thrust—of the business. Whether you have decided to strike out in new directions or have simply refurbished an old mission statement, do not try to paper over differences among individuals by stating generalities or using ambiguous words. That is not only a cop-out but an invitation to internecine struggle that can make substantial progress extremely difficult if it does not destroy the organization completely. Nothing enervates an enterprise more thoroughly than leaders who are pulling against each other. When you see announcements of executive resignations because of "policy differences," in nine out of ten cases the differences are over the proper definition of the nature of the business. When such differences occur at high levels in an organization, there is no solution other than the elimination of the less powerful of the differing parties. Sweeping the differences under the rug is no solution. Neither is a sloppy mission statement.

Your mission team is also the group to review policies. In fact, this planning team might accurately be called the policy-level management. Its members are the "wise men." We will take up policies in the next chapter. But first a word about strategic business units.

Segmentation

If you have been segmenting your business into strategic business units (SBUs) for planning purposes, this is a good time to review the definition of the SBUs. Have they proved to be logically and operationally viable? Maybe you should redefine. Are the SBUs "manageable"? Is it possible to implement a strategy for an SBU the way you are currently organized? Maybe you should consider modifying the organization (more on that in Chapter 4). Are your SBUs still in balance? Is more than 50 percent of your business in one SBU? Can you—should you—split it up? Have you withdrawn from one business area, or has it dried up to the point that it represents only a few percent of your business? Probably it is not worth the paperwork to plan a separate strategy for it. Dump it into "others." Has one of your development projects taken root, and does it look like it wants to go? Maybe it warrants separate attention in its own SBU.

If you are not using SBUs, you should consider it. And now is the time, and your strategy committee is the group for such consideration. How you do it is discussed in Chapter 4.

For Additional Information

Abell, D. F., *Defining the Business: The Starting Point of Strategic Planning.* (Englewood Cliffs, N.J., Prentice-Hall, 1980).

An academic, theoretical treatment of the subject, but well laid out with good practical examples. Starts with the premise, "Defining the business is . . . the most important strategic question that general managers confront since it provides a context within which all other strategic questions can be considered." When he says "business," he is referring to what we have called SBUs.

Pascarella, P., "Is Your Mission Clear?" *Industry Week* (November 14, 1983), pp. 75–77.

A good concise treatment of the formulation of a corporate mission. Talks about such things as "superordinate goals," which is pretty elegant, but don't let it throw you. Says the process "may take two or three months," which unfortu-

nately could be right but impractical. Better to refine it over a period of years.

South, S. E., "Competitive Advantage: The Cornerstone of Strategic Thinking," *Journal of Business Strategy* (Spring 1981), pp. 15–25.

Credits the Japanese as being the masters of competitive positioning.

3
Policing Policies

policy n : *prudence or wisdom in the management of affairs; sagacity; shrewdness*

—*WEBSTER'S COLLEGIATE DICTIONARY*

How are you coming with your policy structure? Bet you had trouble differentiating between policies and objectives. Policies are rules, constraints, limitations on the freedom of decision. Laws, if you will. Notice that *policy* has the same etymological source as *police*. Objectives are accomplishments that you intend to achieve at some fixed point in the future.

If 70 percent of your profits are coming from business with one customer, it is meaningless to have a policy that you will not be dependent on any one customer for more than one-third of your profits. The policy is nonoperational. You could, though, set an objective to reduce your dependence on that customer to no more than 50 percent of your profits within three years. Then you would have to come up with some ideas to make this happen: Toughen up your price negotiations with that customer; take some marginally profitable but stable business in order to provide a flywheel; make an acquisition; put another segment of your business under forced draft to buy volume; whatever.

When you achieve that three-year objective, *then* you can have a policy to never let yourself get that dependent on a single customer again. Or you could set another three-year objective to get the percentage of dependency down to 30 percent and then set out to make it happen.

You can run into the same kind of situation if you are unhappy with your debt/equity ratio or with your margin on sales. You can have a policy of not taking any sales with a net margin of less than 10 percent, but it is meaningless to have a policy to have an average net margin of 15 percent. In the first case, you have a rule that tells you what you can or cannot do. In the second case, you have a standard that you want to achieve, but you will have to work at it in a number of ways. Stating an average margin figure is not likely to dictate a decision in any individual instance.

Rules of Action

Which comes to the heart of the matter. Policies are prefabricated decisions. They are decisions made once and for all to apply in certain specific situations. If they do not provide clear guidance as to what should or should not be done in a specific instance, they lose their function. That is why such words as *encourage, favor, avoid* tend to emasculate policy statements. They leave too much scope for interpretation. "It is our policy to encourage every individual in our organization to realize his or her maximum potential." That is a noble sentiment and it may even be true, but it does not provide much direction for individual management action. If you really mean it, you will be much better served by: "As a matter of policy, we will maintain an ongoing in-house training program for all levels of personnel," or "It is our policy to provide financial support to all employees for job-related educational activities."

If you are going to spend the time trying to crystallize the collective management wisdom of your organization into formal policy statements, take a little additional time to consider the actionable consequences of the policies. Maybe you can think of ways to state your intentions in a form that relates directly to certain kinds of action decisions.

What do you do with the observation, "That's our policy all right, but I wouldn't want to put it in writing"? That's a tough one. One option is to put it in writing all right but keep the corporation's basic strategic policy structure very confidential and limit availability to a small number of top executives. You could publish a deodorized version as a "corporate creed" or some such. A lot of companies do something like this anyhow because their actual policies provide a key to their competitive strategy. But you lose some of the directional advantages of a firm policy position with this option since the lower levels of management obviously cannot follow policies they don't know about. And of course all the "company confidential" stamps in the world will not shield the documents from a subpoena. To some extent, the question is one of management style—how open, how participative, is the management? Or it may just be a matter of paranoia. If a company has an antiunion policy, it is not going to be a secret from much of anybody, and whether it is written down or not is probably irrelevant, even from a legal point of view.

If the policy is legal, that is. It is often said that you do not need to have a policy to obey the law. With the proliferation of laws and regulations, that statement is a little simplistic. It can even be contended that today there is no way you can obey *all* the laws. If you are pursuing an illegal policy, obviously you are not going to record that fact anywhere. But there is compliance and compliance. You can commit yourself to meeting all environmental protection standards, or you can comply when forced to after all judicial delays have been exhausted. The same can be said for the enactments of the Occupational Safety and Health Administration, the Equal Employment Opportunity Commission, wage and hour regulations, the Corrupt Practices Act, and many others. These are all appropriate areas for establishing policy.

In fact, it is commonly believed that there is some prophylactic value in having stated policies in such areas as corrupt practices, pricing actions, and so on. Then when the underlying gets caught off base, the top brass can do a Pontius

Pilate and say, "He knew the corporate policy forbade such activities, and so we have no responsibility." That reasoning has proven a pretty permeable shield in a great many cases, but it still is probably worth making corporate policy in these matters explicit—particularly if you mean it.

What about policies directly related to matters of ethics? Fairness to suppliers? Employees? Obligations to the country and the community? Contribution to science or to an industry? Some managements feel very strongly and sincerely about such matters and want their positions to be on record. From an operational point of view, though, they are better incorporated in a corporate creed or statement of principles. This can be highly pertinent and still stated in general or philosophical terms. Reserve your policy structure for actionable statements that give specific decision-making guidance. Keep the distinction clean. However, you may very well have specific policies that implement some of the principles declared in the creed.

Enforcement

Which brings us to the question of how do you enforce policies? What if they are being widely ignored? Ultimately, this becomes a matter of organizational discipline that is beyond the scope of this book, but there are a few procedural things that you can do. The first thing is to write your policies in unambiguous terms so that there is never any argument as to whether a particular action is or is not in accord with policy. If there are loopholes, you can be sure that someone will try to crawl through them. The second, of course, is to make sure that appropriate people know about and understand policies. We have already observed that people cannot follow policies they do not know about. But even if policies are disseminated appropriately, it should be done with some ceremony or they will end up in a file somewhere. Some companies send out policy statements in duplicate every year with the request that the second copy be returned dated and signed "read and understood." This is particularly desirable with policies having legal implications but is not a bad idea in any case. It may provide more psychological comfort, though, than actual legal protection.

Ultimately, of course, the chief executive officer is responsible for conformance to policy, as he or she is for everything else, but it is sometimes useful to designate other individuals to police specific policies and possibly to report annually on conformance, impact, and exceptions. The finance officer can be responsible for financial policy, the human resources officer for personnel policies, and so on.

In trying to police policies, you will run into certain types of reactions:

• The *maverick* just cannot seem to remember to conform to policies. Says, "Gee whiz, I forgot" after the fact. Your maverick may be just a case of arrested adolescence, in which case perhaps you should suggest that he or she would be happier in a less adult environment. On the other hand, the person may be a certifiable genius—technical, marketing, production, entrepreneurial—in which case you want to hang on to him or her. However, you had better find a way to insulate the rest of the enterprise from this unorthodox influence. Set up a "skunk works," set up a subsidiary, spin off a new venture under contract. Quite often a really innovative free spirit can make things work in very unconventional ways. The trouble is, if you allow such a person a great deal of freedom within an organization, a lot of other people with much less talent will demand or assume equal license, often with disastrous results.

• The *old maid* lives by the motto "a place for everything, and everything in its place." Wants a policy to cover every contingency. Your best bet is to rely on peer pressure. Point out that policies are essential principles of management on which everyone can agree. If this person can not build a consensus, the policy proposal must be tabled.

• The *old-timer* was here before there were policies—therefore policies are fine for the youngsters but do not apply to him or her. Appeal to this person's special responsibility for leadership. Point out the provisions for orderly exceptions to policy—but gently, gently. The old-timer may not be around that much longer anyhow.

• The *politician* comes around after the meeting to tell the

CEO about the hot new deal he or she has, which the other managers would not understand, but that requires a deviation from policy. Tell the politician to put the idea in writing and you will take it up at the next meeting. This one you must deal with very firmly.

• The *armadillo* will try to stretch policy to cover unrelated situations so as to avoid independent decisions. This type of person may become more prevalent as policy structures become more extensive. The armadillo often makes common cause with an old maid. This is a particularly difficult attitude to change. Probably the best response is to put the person in a position that does not require many policy-level decisions.

If you find that certain policies are being violated frequently, either through formal exceptions or surreptitiously, it may mean that you have a chaotic management. However, it is just as likely that for some reason the policy is inappropriate. Remember, policies are merely those decisions that everyone agrees constitute a wise and prudent way to run the business. If such agreement obviously does not exist, then scrap the policy. It will not take any more time to deal on a case-by-case basis with the situations as they arise than constantly to make exceptions to policy, and your management will have a lot more credibility. Just don't kid yourself that you have a policy if you really do not. "Honesty is the best policy," particularly when it comes to writing policies.

What about exceptions to policy? Obviously, you need an escape hatch to avoid foolish rigidity. In a strict legalistic sense, once policies have been approved by the board of directors, only they can authorize violations of the rules. This is seldom practicable, nor is it often practiced. Most commonly this authority is delegated either explicitly or implicitly to the CEO. However, to impose this responsibility on a single person exposes him or her to tremendous personal and organizational pressure (e.g., from the "politician"). If the policy was significant in the first place, it is unlikely that a decision to evade it will have to be made in a matter of a few days. It is much more desirable to defer the exception decision to the group whose consensus created the policy in the first place. This group will usually be the planning committee or the executive committee. In some companies, it will literally be called the "policy committee" or simply "the policy-level management."

In Retrospect

This is a good time to look back over the record of your existing policies. Over the past three or four years, did they really make any difference? Is there some deadwood in there whose purpose is strictly decorative? Or, more likely, are some of the policies stated in such fuzzy terms that they can be interpreted almost any way anyone wants to read them? Can you harden them up by restating them so that they really provide a go/no-go gauge? Have some of the policies been followed conscientiously but the results were not really that good? Maybe you were not as smart as you thought you were when you set them and you should reconsider. Maybe some of them are just plain silly. On the other hand, have you learned anything in the past four or five years, perhaps painfully? Do you want to establish a policy to prevent getting in that particular crack again?

Certainly you should not let your strategic policies swing around like a weathervane. But neither should they be cut so deeply into the rock that once established they become eternal verities never to be questioned. Remember, as Mr. Webster says, policies are the codification of management's prudence and wisdom, their sagacity and shrewdness. As you get older, you should get wiser.

Keep clearly in mind *why* you have policies. Their function is to speed up decision making and to keep you out of trouble. If they are not doing that, there is something wrong; they are not working.

If you are having trouble establishing a coherent policy structure, maybe it is because the people involved lack a consistent image of the company. A company that says it has no formal policies very often in fact has more pseudopolicies than anybody else. "Everybody knows the way we do it." Everybody is making policy. The trouble is that they may not all be making the *same* policies. If you suspect this might be a problem, it would be worthwhile to do a little poll with a form like the one in Figure 2. It is what is called a semantic differential test, and you will want people to complete it quickly, instinctively, without too much conscious thought. It is primarily to get a reaction to words, but the words will reflect a person's perception of corporate policies and practices. While you are at it, you may as well ask people to express their agreement or disagreement with the way things are done around the shop. Ask them to indicate what they think the policies are and also the way they would like to see them.

You can do this poll among just your top management or as far down the organization as you want to go. It depends on where you think the problem is. To get the most meaningful results, have the forms returned unsigned.

If you get a wide spread of responses on existing policies, there is confusion in the ranks. You either have a communications problem, or people are indeed marching to a bunch of different drummers. Either way, you had better take some steps to straighten out their perceptions.

If you get a wide spread between existing and desired policies, you have a different kind of problem—a tougher one.

(Text continues on page 36.)

Figure 2.   Semantic differential test for polling employee perception of and attitude toward corporate policies.

> This poll is intended to record your instinctive reaction to *words*. Do not take a great deal of time checking definitions or analyzing your responses.
>
> First, make a check (✓) in one of the eight segments of the line to indicate where you think the character of your company falls between the two terms shown. If neither applies, check the middle segment. If one of the terms is meaningless for your company, check the other end of the scale.
>
> Now go back through the form and place an X on each scale to show the character you would like to see your company acquire.
>
> We are not concerned with public image. Do not consider what outsiders may think about the company or what you would like them to think. We are concerned about what *you* think about the company you work for.

Operations

Know-how		Scientific
Cost Conscious		"Get the Job Done"
Traditional		Modern Methods
"Can Do"		Planned
Flexible Equipment		Specialized Equipment
Steady Work Load		Variable Work Load
High-Pressure Work Pace		Uniform Work Pace
Close Supervision		Standardized Procedures
Complex Operations		Simple Operations

Finance

Large Capital Requirements		Fast Money Turnover
Conservative Accounting		Modern Money Management
Flexible Budget		Firm Budget
Small Profit, Low Risk		High Profit, High Risk
High Leverage		Conservative Debt
Assets Management		Operations Management

Human Resources

Seniority	Achievement
Brilliance	Dependability
Company Employee Development	Individual Self-Development
Personal Involvement	"Day's Work for a Day's Pay"
Paternal	Modern Fringe Benefits
Motivation	Supervision
Teamwork	Individuality
Professional	Personal

Marketing

Regular Customers	Transient Clientele
Price Oriented	Service Oriented
Dignified	Promotional
Businesslike	Personable
Hard Sell	Soft Sell
Stand Behind Product	"You Get What You Pay For"

Corporate Strategy

Adventurous		Specialized
Orderly		Quick
Defensive		Offensive
Responsive		Initiators
Predictable Environment		Hectic Environment
Opportunism		Stability

Organization

Watch How They Do It		Measure Results Only
Spontaneous		Organized
Centralized		Decentralized
Personal		Impersonal
"The Boss Decides"		Delegation to Professional Managers
Defined Responsibilities		Flexible

Some real soul searching is in order to decide whether you should actually change the way things are done or change people's attitudes about the way things are done. Neither alternative is going to be easy.

Lost Horizons

You may have included in your policy structure the statement: "We will maintain and implement a five-year strategic plan." It always does a planning consultant's heart good to see such a commitment. But is five years the right planning reach for you? With a number of years' planning experience now under your belt, you should have a pretty good feel for it. But just to check that feel, let's go back over the following exercise, which you should have done when you first picked your planning period.

	Number of years
Time from new product concept to market introduction	_____
Time from new plant decision to on-stream	_____
Average life of product model	_____
Average life of process technology	_____
Pay-back period on major equipment	_____
Time required to reach target market penetration with new product or market	_____

You obviously cannot plan out to the longest period on this list. It is equally obvious that plans that do not extend beyond the shortest period will be meaningless, and you should go at least a year beyond that. If I had to pick a single determining parameter to set the planning period, it would be the new product cycle for a rapidly growing company and the pay-back period for a more mature one. But in specific instances, your business sense will tell you how to compromise among these considerations.

There are also what you might call "operational" considerations in setting a planning horizon, which arise from the operation of the planning process itself. When you first got into planning, you may have found that your associates, all structural considerations notwithstanding, were uncomfortable. They felt silly dealing with speculations about events in time dimensions of five years or more. This is a very common reaction.

The response is frequently to settle for a three-year plan. Sometimes this is done explicitly as a learning exercise. "When we get comfortable with three-year planning, we can stretch it out to four or five years." That is a reasonable expedient, and sometimes it works. Unfortunately, it usually doesn't. The reason it doesn't work is that the initial uneasiness almost always arises from a misapprehension about the nature of planning and three-year planning is only too likely to reinforce that misconception.

The root problem is a confusion between *planning* and *forecasting*. You have read it hundreds of times: "Planning is deciding where you want to get to and then deciding what you have to do to get there." But it does not sink in. Forecasting specific events five years or more in the future on the basis of present knowledge and trends may indeed be a futile effort. But planning does not work that way. Planning works from ends to means. It starts with an act of will—a determination that certain results will be attained—and then considers the various ways in which those ends might be achieved. It fully accepts the fact that all the intervening events are not predictable. But it focuses attention on the goal to be achieved, with frank expectation that tactics will have to be modified from time to time to accommodate unforeseen events. That is why plans are revised every year. Planning does not presume either prescience or omniscience. It does presume commitment to the achievement of certain results. It does require a certain kind of courage, but the objection that no one knows what will happen in five years is inappropriate and hence irrelevant. The whole purpose of planning is to *make* it happen, to become a driver and not a passenger.

There is nothing inherently wrong with three-year plans. They can be completely results oriented, true strategic plans. In certain industries with short development cycles and quick response times, they can be quite adequate and in fact the only practical course. The trouble is that they look too much like a budget and may become essentially a three-year budget, a three-year extrapolation of current operations. Such an extrapolation can be useful, particularly when it illuminates the serious consequences of the continuation of some existing trends. But it is not really a *strategic* plan. And if it really is only a three-year budget, maybe a computer could do it better, or faster, or cheaper.

So if you are making a three-year, "long-range" plan, do some soul searching. Is it really a statement of committed intent, or is it merely an extrapolation? And if it is truly a plan, does it reach far enough out to give you enough leverage to achieve significant changes in the nature of the business?

Outpost Year

Even if you decide that a three-year plan is right for you, or a five-year plan for that matter, you should be ready for a little mind stretching. Add an "outpost year" to your plan. If it is a three-year plan, go out five years. If it is a five-year plan, go out eight or ten years. What do you want the enterprise to look like at that time: How big in sales? In assets? What kind of product mix? What geographic market coverage? You are not going to flesh these numbers out in great detail or justify them with a lot of specifics. If somebody calls them wishful thinking or blue sky, don't get too upset. Just tell them, "A person has to dream!" But you know that if you do it right you can make these things happen. And if your whole management team is convinced they can make them happen, by golly, there is a good chance that they will happen.

There is a trick that the futurists use that you might want to try in conjunction with your outpost year. They call it "future history." Here is what you do. You pretend that you are out in that future year, maybe at your retirement banquet. All these good things have been accomplished and you are bragging about how you did it: what you did first, what you did next, and how it all worked out. This is just another way of writing a scenario, but by turning the time frame around, it attempts to break the habit of extrapolative thinking.

And that is the principal reason for setting an outpost year. By consciously skipping a few intervening years, you try to break the trend-line projection. Let's be honest. Some people will cheat on you, but you can try. It also gives you an aiming point. You can draw a figurative line from "now" to that far out future date and see if your current strategies will keep you somewhere near that line. In other words, will what you are planning to do really get you where you want to go?

I must confess that a lot of managers, as they become more adept at planning, begin to fill in behind their outpost until it becomes, in fact, the final year of their formal plan. That's all right. On the other hand, if you have been making five-year plans but the outer years are a formality with no sense of realism about them, drop back to a three-year plan, but keep that fifth year as an outpost year.

The Planning Base

Now you have your planning base. This was the purpose of these first sessions. If as the result of these sessions you have modified your mission, this is a major change and you will want to get the word around right away. It probably warrants a convocation of the next level of management beyond those that participated in the decision. They deserve an explanation of how the direction or the scope of the enterprise will be changed and why this decision was made. You can try to do it with a memorandum, but if you do, you had better be a very skillful and persuasive writer.

Presumably your marketing people are in the process of updating their market analysis. They have to know quickly that the ground rules have changed and that the market has been redefined. Usually, though, a marketing person will have been at the strategy sessions and will carry that message directly and undertake to modify the analytical scheme.

If there have been changes in policy, these usually can be disseminated in writing, supplemented with some one-on-one discussion with those directly involved. Of course, if you have a meeting to discuss the mission, you can explain any policy changes at that time.

Establishing SBUs or redefining existing SBUs requires a

good deal of explaining, which should be handled carefully to be sure that anybody who will be involved understands what is going on. If there are to be organizational changes, you will handle those, of course, like you would any other change in assignments.

If as the result of your critique of past planning performance you decide to alter your planning procedure, you will have to issue some kind of new planning guide. This is necessary even for those who were present at the strategy sessions because the decisions must be translated into operational terms. If you have a planning coordinator, this is his or her job. Otherwise, the CEO had better do it personally. Have you changed the planning horizon? Upgraded the quality of some of the inputs? Or just changed the emphasis and way in which some of the inputs are to be used? In any case, this is the time to send out the planning calendar for the year, and a little introductory philosophizing about special needs and emphasis is certainly in order.

For Additional Information

King, W. R., and Cleland, D. I., *Strategic Planning and Policy.* New York: Van Nostrand Reinhold Company, 1978.

The title is somewhat misleading. There really is not much good literature on policy—probably because it is so subjective.

4
Environmentalism

The world is so full of a number of things, I'm sure we should all be as happy as kings.

—ROBERT LOUIS STEVENSON

As planning processes become more sophisticated, they inevitably devote an increasing portion of their efforts to analysis of the environment. There are at least two reasons for this tendency. The first and most obvious is that the more you know, the more you know you don't know. By a sort of simple geometry, as you expand the field of your knowledge of what is going on around you, the perimeter of that field where the knowledge ends and the ignorance begins gets larger and larger. You can never know everything you would like to know about your business environment. The temptation to learn just a little more is almost irresistible.*

*An interesting sidelight on this reaction: A research study of 26 Canadian and 36 U.S. corporations found that the firms that were successful in terms of growth and profitability increased their analytical activity when the environment became unsettled and the competition more "hostile." The unsuccessful companies did just the opposite, flailing around and trying anything. D. Miller and P. H. Friesen, "Strategy Making and Environment," *Strategic Management Journal*, Vol. 4 (1983), pp. 221–235.

The second and more subtle reason is that, as a planning system gets run in and begins to operate smoothly, it becomes capable of absorbing and effectively utilizing more and more input data. If you do not have the machinery to process it, additional input may become merely an information overload and a source of confusion. Once you know how to use it, the appetite for information increases substantially.

There is often a third reason, which is not so constructive. If you have any professional planners around, you will have learned that they are obsessed with curiosity about what is going on. If you do not watch them, they will build an analytical empire that will not only bust the budget but inundate the management.

By now you should have your environmental inputs organized to some degree, but it is quite possible that you are more frustrated with them than you were when you didn't know you wanted them. Perhaps it is time for an upgrade.

Market Analysis

How are you making out with your market information? A lot depends on what happened the first time you asked the sales manager for a market forecast as opposed to a sales forecast. If you got a panicky "There aren't any data for our industry," you have probably had problems. Actually, these days some data exist on almost any industry. In the past ten years, the multiclient studies have become ubiquitous and some of the security houses have begun to make their industry studies publicly available—at a price. The odds are excellent that somebody in the past couple of years has studied what you would like to know. There are several directories of such studies listed by subject (see "For Additional Information" at the end of the chapter).

The data in the multiclient studies are not always reliable, and it is ordinarily good insurance to check back with the author (usually a freelancer) to find out just how the breakdown categories were defined. The prices of off-the-shelf multiclient studies have been escalating, and they are now almost all over $1,000, but even so, they are still a quick, inexpensive way to get a start on any market study. After all, you do not have to save many days' time, travel, and phone expense to add up to $1,000.

Then, of course, there are all the contract market research outfits and the subscription studies by such institutions as Battelle and SRI International, and the trade associations, and the government offices, and on and on. No, the "There are no data" excuse just will not wash.

If you have a marketing manager or product managers, you should not have run into this problem, but if you are still relying on a field sales force to forecast the markets for you, you may very well experience some frustration. You are not the first. Let's face it. Good salespeople are not often good analysts. They are busy; they have their eyes on getting the next order and on their performance bonuses. They usually are enthusiastic and emotional. That is the way you want them, but they get impatient and feel imposed upon if you ask them for too much market information.

The Product Manager

After all, the institution of the product manager came into being because somebody had to step back and look at the broad opportunities for developing the product line while other people took care of the day-to-day making and selling. You may want to consider some kind of product manager set-up. A lot of organizations have evolved in this fashion. Planning and strategizing business segments tend to spawn product managers. You will want to be very careful, though, how you set up such a position. There are a lot of different jobs that are done under the title "product manager," so the management literature may be a little confusing. The jobs range from management trainees, who do a lot of miscellaneous staff and liaison work, to virtual czars, who set prices, schedule the plant, supervise product development and technical service, and have bottom-line responsibility. In one-product line companies, a marketing manager has essentially the functions of a product manager.

The primary consideration is to delineate clearly the interactions between the product manager and the other functional managers. If you are going to venture into a product management setup, you had better establish it initially as a strictly staff function: analyzing, coordinating, expediting, but not deciding. This will create problems, and the designee, particularly if he or she is any good, will suffer many frustrations, but it is usually the only practical option. Pick your candidate in anticipation of these problems. Then put it all on the table in front of this person. The product manager must be analytical but imaginative, forceful but diplomatic, and above all a negotiator. And sometimes this person is going to feel impatient, unappreciated, and just plain mad.

Start the product manager out to get the market pegged down. This will not only provide substantive data but also serve for his or her personal orientation. It may also generate the first confrontation. What if the market data will not justify the sales forecast? Or, worse yet, indicate that the sales projections are overly modest? What if the feedback from the market destroys some passionately believed myths of the sales force? The product is *not* primarily an impulse purchase. Competitor A is doing much better than anyone thought because he is serving a different segment of the market. The product is doing fine but will almost certainly be technologically obsolete within two or three years. Ideally, these discrepancies can be reconciled off-line between sales and marketing.

Sales Versus Marketing

But what if they aren't? Much of the logic of your whole plan structure depends on the credibility of the sales projections. If your top managers do not believe in these projections, they will hedge their commitment to the plan. If you impose a sales forecast on your salespeople, then it is your forecast, not theirs, and you will probably lose their commitment. It's a real dilemma.

If the sales department is adamant, disputes the market facts, and insists on its numbers, you probably have no choice but to accept them. Your only real option is to subscribe to the German industrialist Frederick Flick's dictum, "Change the numbers or change the faces." If you accept the numbers, you must make it abundantly clear that sales is on the hook for the promised performance—no second quesses permitted. You must then track the actual sales performance to see if it reflects the indicated dynamics of the market and is not just a fortuitous coincidence of compensating errors. The divergence between the two estimates is probably not too great in the first year anyway. The big gaps arise in the more distant, strategic years. By the next planning cycle, the differences may begin to resolve themselves. If they do not and you continue to get unreliable sales forecasts, you have a staffing problem, which was not created but merely illuminated by having better market information. You can either "change the faces" or shift greater responsibilty to the marketing (or product) manager. When you reviewed your past planning performance, how did the sales forecast hold up?

If you encounter this kind of schism between sales and marketing, it will be difficult to avoid an adversary relationship between the individuals involved. You can do what you can to minimize this reaction, but since if you are forced to a choice you must go with the salespeople, the product manager will inevitably suffer the frustration that you warned comes with the territory.

To some extent, you will institutionalize this adversary situation by reviewing the market analysis at the very beginning of the next set of planning sessions. The entire planning committee, including sales management, gets a chance to ask questions, raise objections, make suggestions, and nobody leaves the room until there is general acceptance of the analysis—possibly as modified—as realistic and realizable. Then, if the eventual sales objectives are related back to the market dynamics, there is less likelihood that some key people will think the sales objectives are a lot of blue sky.

Eventually you may want to set up market research as a separate function, because, to be honest, a good solid market analyst does not always have the imagination to fully exploit a product line. You can locate this function organizationally in one of a number of places, but from what has been said above, the one place you do not want to put it is in the sales department. That is like putting quality control under manufacturing.

After being initiated by conducting market studies, your product manager can begin to broaden his or her scope. Coordination of the planning and production of advertising and promotional materials is usually something the manager can take on without undue controversy unless there is trouble with an in-house advertising department. New product planning will require close interaction with the research and development department.

New Product Introduction

Whether or not you put new product introduction, sometimes called "commercial development," directly under the product manager is a watershed decision. If you do, this person now has direct responsibility for tangible results. If the product manager identified the market, guided the design of the product, and developed the promotional appeal, he or she ought to be willing to sell it. At least there will be no one else to blame if it flops. You also avoid diverting the regular sales force from its ongoing sales activities, educating your representatives to the virtues of the new product, building their enthusiasm, and probably having to provide some kind of incentive compensation to make it worth their while to spend their time educating customers to the point where they will place an order. Eventually, of course, at some preestablished point—a certain sales volume, a cost break-even, a share of market—you will add the new product to the sales department's regular product line.

Keeping new product introductions out of the sales department has a lot to recommend it. However, once you give a product manager some operating responsibilities, those responsibilities will probably expand. He or she is likely to take on business development activities, the acquisition of additional product lines or even companies, contract production or packaging outside the company, licensing arrangements, and who knows what else. You are on the way to making the product manager a very important person—which perhaps is just what you had in mind.

For a small or a one-product company, everything that has just been said about product managers also applies to a marketing manager position set up separately from the direct selling activity. The advantages are there to be realized. But so are the frustrations.

Whether or not you go to a product manager setup—or, if you're a one-product company, appoint a marketing manager separate from sales—commit some good resources to exploring the nature of your markets. Management experts have been saying for generations: "Know your markets." It has been demonstrated time and again that the most successful companies in an industry are the ones with the most intimate communications with their customers—that know where their customers are coming from and where they are going; that know why people buy a given product. Obviously, some people are learning the lesson better than others. If you can learn it well, no other one input will contribute as much to planned success.

Strategic Business Units (SBUs)

The whole concept of product management presupposes that you have segmented your business into several product lines. Segmentation of markets or businesses goes back to the very beginnings of market research. Market analysts discovered early on that they could get a much better grasp of the characteristics of a market, and therefore could be more accurate, if they broke it down into subunits based on applications, or geographics, or price ranges—almost any breakdown that made some kind of logical sense. Now they do it reflexively as a matter of routine.

It was not until the 1960s, though, that the concept began to be extended to planning and devising strategies. Profit centers had become quite common by then, but they were largely based in budgeting. The unit president concept was gaining some currency but was usually considered in an organizational context associated with decentralization. General Electric probably pioneered with business segment strategies, although these things are always hard to trace. The American Management Associations' Center for Planning and Implementation at that time called these segments simply *subbusinesses,* but GE called them, more elegantly, *strategic business units.* That nomenclature has pretty much prevailed, although you do hear other terms, such as *strategic planning units.*

In my earlier book, I dealt with such business segmentation rather lightly to avoid unnecessary complexity. However, since that was written in 1976, the whole portfolio management approach has gained so much attention that some further comments are undoubtedly in order.

First of all, the technique of segmenting a company's business into several more or less homogeneous components for purposes of strategic planning is sound for the very practical reason that it enables managers to come to more intimate grips with the business decisions that must be made. It works. It helps you to see situations more sharply and to determine what is going on and what is likely to go on in the future. No business is a monolithic chunk. Even in a relatively simple business, managers will usually gain more precise perceptions and make more pertinent decisions if they break the overall strategy decision into more closely focused units.

Segmentation provides a more positive grip on the business, enables you to deploy your limited resources more effectively, and probably makes things less confusing and frustrating. The little extra planning effort is a good investment. Some people say it doesn't work in some kinds of job-shop operations, but even job shops usually have more than one source of business, more than one market. In a one-product, start-up situation that is scrambling for its life—let's face it, there is probably no time for strategic planning anyway. The pure one-product, one-market company is really quite rare and, when it does occur, probably has so little strategic flexibility that long-range planning is inappropriate. One-product companies can often get considerable management leverage by setting up SBUs on a regional basis or by size of account or some other dimension unrelated to product category.

In a complex business, segmentation is essential. Products are in different stages of their life cycles. Competitive environments vary. The pace of change is not the same across the board. The cost/price relationships are not the same. Uniform strategy applied to all parts of the business would have to be a compromise, and quite likely a bad one. Segmentation is absolutely necessary to get anything like optimal results.

However, segmentation is only a useful tool, not a magic wand. Dealing in strategic business units is very helpful. Trying to cram SBUs into simplistic categories based on zoological grids is not. What does it tell you? "Back your winners." "Cut your losses." "Don't beat your head against a brick wall." Those cliches have been around for a long time. So what else is new?

Unfortunately, these gimmicky, black-box formulations have given strategy a bad name. That's too bad. Strategy is a great concept. Being in the right place at the right time with the right resources is still more than half the battle—sometimes all of it. I consciously avoided the term in my earlier book because it was already taking on iconographic overtones at the time I was writing. But the fact remains that the great strategists from Karl von Clausewitz to Alfred Sloan to Tom Watson knew the secret of success.

So use SBUs. Think strategically. But don't try shortcuts with patented nostrums.

How Do You Do It?

How do you set up SBUs? How do you define them? It depends pretty much on how you see the business, how you intend to run it. They can be delineated by product lines, but not necessarily. Sometimes it makes more sense to do it by raw material or kind of technology. You can do it by kinds of markets or channels of distribution. In some kinds of businesses geography is the best parameter. In multinational companies that is often the only option that works. Some service companies find it very useful to segment by size of accounts. What you want to do is pick out units that could under some other circumstances be run as separate businesses with definable markets, discrete economic characteristics, and a coherent environment.

How many SBUs should you have? Not more than you can handle! For most people that means not more than 12. You get bogged down in too many details, too many numbers, with more than that. Six or eight is better. Three or four may be enough for a smaller company. Don't be misled when you read that Union Carbide has 60 SBUs or GE has 120. It's a matter of nomenclature. Yes, somebody strategizes all of those businesses separately, but not top management. Top managers deal in groups, usually four, five, or six. It is just a matter of human capacity. Your mind can encompass only so many variants.

If your initial impulse is to set up a whole lot of SBUs, you'll have to find some rational basis for aggregation. What can be combined with what? Put like with like until you get a practical number. Any part of the business that does not provide more than 5 percent of sales or of profits probably does not warrant treatment as a separate SBU. The exception would be a fledgling activity that is expected to grow rapidly and have a great future. Otherwise, put the odds and ends in an "other" SBU, collect the proper numbers there, but don't bother to plan strategy separately.

Once you have agreed upon the proper segmentation of your business, you must decide what the market is for each SBU. This is like defining a mission on a smaller scale. For each SBU, you must decide where and with whom you will contend for what market. As with a mission decision, this is not an exclusionary definition; it does not say you will turn down any sales anywhere. It merely says where you will actively and aggressively compete. The definition may be made by the top management or, if you are organized according to SBUs, by the people responsible for the SBUs. But it should be made very thoughtfully and collegially by everybody involved in the planned performance. It should not be made authoritatively. This is a committee job.

Let's admit it. There is a certain amount of circular reasoning involved here. You cannot identify your competitors until you designate the arena in which you will compete. But you cannot rationally decide what your competitive market scope is until you know what the competition is. Don't let it bug you. If you have been planning for five years, you know that this sort of paradox arises all the time. Theoretically, it is difficult. Practically, you can deal with it. If you need a fancy way of saying it, you make a series of successive approximations.

Share of Market

Everything you have heard about the Profit Impact of Market Share (PIMS)* is more or less true. Also for experience curves, which are in effect the same thing. What is usually not pointed out is that you can delineate the market you have a share of. That delineation is the most important decision. You cannot talk about competition until you declare who your competitors are. You cannot talk about market shares until you decide what market you are sharing. Until you define the market, your discussions are going to be fuzzy and inconclusive. You want a market in which you can be a significant factor.

You want a market where you have a recognizable special character—a unique advantage, if possible. You want a market that you can service adequately with the resources at your disposal. Particularly, you want a market where you can make money, which is to say one in which you are at least as favorably positioned as the competitors. This is what niche strategies are all about. There are big niches and little niches, but you must choose the area in which you are going to compete—and then compete there and not somewhere else. You don't care about the technical capabilities or the distribution strengths of someone if you do not intend to go toe-to-toe with him or her anyway.

As a rough rule of thumb, the old 10 percent is a good place to start. In most competitive arenas, you will have difficulty competing effectively if you have less than 10 percent of the market. In some industries, particularly highly fragmented ones, the rule does not work. If nobody has 10 percent of the market, obviously you do not need 10 percent to compete. On the other hand, some supermarket chains say

*In the earlier book this work was credited to the Market Science Institute at Harvard Business School. It has since been spun off as the freestanding Strategic Planning Institute.

that they must have 40 percent of a served market to be competitive under current conditions.

You may want to use a relative market share target. There are a number of such formulas, and they all tell you more or less the same thing. One commonly used is to compare your market share with that of your four largest competitors. The usual target figure is 50 percent. If they have 40 percent among them, you should have 20 percent to be a strong competitor. That's a pretty high hurdle rate, and maybe it's too high. Some analysts think you are all right if you have 20 percent of the share of the top five suppliers, which may or may not include you. These formulas are most applicable in fragmented markets.

The arithmetic on relative market shares works out the same whether you use market share percentages or actual dollar volumes. Relative market share calculations have the minor advantage that you can do them without knowing the total market volume. You only need to know the performance of the top suppliers. In any case, you should not take these theoretical numbers too literally. Obviously, it is not a case of 10 percent you are in, 9 percent you are out. But the idea that you should concentrate your resources in such a way that you can establish a significant presence in a defined market is important.

Remember, *you* define the market. You manage the business so that the numbers come out right. The numbers do not manage the business. If your company is relatively small, define your market rather narrowly—assume a niche strategy. If you are in a strong relative position, you may want to expand your primary market to broaden the area in which you compete actively. But pick the market so that the share numbers come out in your favor, not the other way around. This may require a series of successive approximations; however, it's not only practical but critical.

Competition

Once you have decided on your SBU market segments, you can turn your analysts loose to determine volumes, trends, applications, major customers, prices—all the usual market information—about each business segment. This is not a book on market research, so we will not go into all the technical details here. But the most important thing to know about your market is who else is in it. It does not matter how good you are if your competitors are better. On the other hand, there is nothing better for a business than a bunch of sloppy competitors. If you do not know anything else about your business environment, you should at least know what your competitors are doing and, if possible, why.

Ask your market analysts to increase their efforts to understand the competition this year. Whether they do it for the overall corporation or by SBU is a matter of common sense. If all the SBUs encounter pretty much the same competitors, the analysis can be done overall and then the SBUs can split out their segments later. If there are a whole bunch of different competitor groups, then each SBU must be dealt with separately. In either case, identify the major suppliers to the market as defined in your corporate mission or in an SBU's charter. The top ten, including yourself, should be enough. Even a football player has to contend with only 11 competitors, and you are unlikely to be able to handle more than that. Put the rest in "others." In a highly fragmented market, "others" may account for 20, 30, or even 40 percent of the sales, but they are probably all mom-and-pop operations with similar characteristics and you can deal with them categorically. Unless you are in cigarettes or breakfast foods or something like that, plus or minus 1 percent market share will be accurate enough to tell you all you want to know.

At this point, the analysts may encounter some systematic problems. In many cases, there will be a certain amount of "captive" market—consumers who make their own material, buy from a sister company, or get the product over the fence in a way that precludes other sources of supply. Be sure you exclude those from your market potential. Talk about "available" or "accessible" market. You cannot base your strategy on potential that is not really there. You could find a situation where total consumption is increasing but the available market is shrinking. Just be sure, though, that the captive market is really inaccessible. Sometimes you can break up those cozy relationships and cause the user to buy outside, but you must have something very special to offer.

What if there is someone on the list of competitors with a sizable chunk of the market who sells a product that serves the same function that yours does but is fundamentally different from what you make? Say you are in the casual furniture business, but you make only wrought iron furniture. What do you do about the people who make all that aluminum or redwood furniture? They may take sales away from you, but you really do not directly compete with them. Their cost/price structure is different. Their channels of distribution are different. You have to rethink your definition of the market. Are you in casual furniture? If you are, you have such a piddling market share that you are going to be hard put to compete effectively. Or are you really in wrought iron furniture, where you are a significant factor in the market?

If you choose the first option, you have set yourself the very major task of competing across the board in that large and complex market. If you take the more limited approach, you pit yourself against the other wrought iron people. Then you classify the tubular aluminum producers as *functional competitors*. You don't ignore them, but you don't go against them head to head. Take your functional competition out of your share of market calculations, and list it separately. You probably will not need to track it company by company. What you do want to know is how it is doing collectively compared to your primary market segment. If its total sales are growing faster than those of the area in which you compete directly, you have a problem.

Some planners go a step beyond functional competitors and look at *economic competition*. What they are looking at is the way vacation travel competes with backyard swimming pools or even how two small cars in a family compete with one big car. But that is probably a little too subtle for us at this point.

There is another kind of problem that you may encounter in looking at market shares. Suppose you are a Canadian company that has 80 percent of your domestic market and 5 percent of a U.S. market that is ten times as large. To say you have 12 percent of the North American market is meaningless. Again you have a problem of defining your primary markets. You have two choices. You can decide that you will compete directly only in the Canadian market and take any U.S. business as marginal sales. However, your U.S. sales are almost as great as your sales in Canada, so what you probably want to do is set up a separate SBU. You have to set it up separately because your competitive position with 5 percent of the market is much different than it is with 80 percent and your whole strategy will be different.

Once you have your primary market nailed down and you know who is supplying it, you want to know who is doing well and who is not. You may not know sales figures for individual competitors, but you should have a pretty good notion of who is gaining share, who is losing share, and who is just hanging in there. Put little arrows next to the share percentages—up for gain, down for loss, horizontal for holding (see Figure 3 in Chapter 5). Now step back and see what you have. Is everybody gaining share? Can't be. This is a zero-sum game. Remember we are talking share, not volume. If someone's sales are not growing as fast as the market, they are losing share. How about you? Are all of the gains being made at the expense of one supplier? That supplier could be in trouble or may be just liquidating his or her position and consciously withdrawing from the market. Are the little guys down in "other" the big losers? The market is consolidating, becoming more concentrated. Already you have learned something.

If you can get your market analysis to extend beyond just volumes, prices, and applications and provide basic information about the status of competitors, your planning time will be much more productive. Some planners do an individual profile on each major competitor, but for a modest-sized company, that may be excessive paperwork. Let the analysis get up to share of market information, and let the senior management take it from there.

Competition has gotten a lot tougher since the last time I wrote on this subject. A Republican administration has made some moves to restore competition in previously sheltered markets. A couple of years of really tough times in some industries has squeezed out a lot of hangers-on. But mostly, for one reason or another, the competition has gotten smarter. There are more professional managers. There is, you will pardon the parochialism, more skillful planning. Market niches do not stay open as long as they used to. Products do not retain their competitive advantage as long. People know what their markets are doing. Marketers are learning to focus their efforts on specific market segments. And customers are getting smarter, too. They no longer will pay for what they do not use. All kinds of products with gold-plated services are being clobbered by stripped-down competitors.

So competitive analysis is getting a lot more attention than it ever did before. One of the most widely read management books of recent years is titled simply *Competitive Strategy.**

Industry Analysis

If your market researchers have got their market data in pretty good shape, you might ask them to do an industry analysis for you. It will be very valuable in eventually setting strategies. What are the general characteristics of the industry in which the SBUs operate? They may vary widely from SBU to SBU.

One of the first things to look at is *ease of entry*. Any business that can be established these days for less than $100,000 of fixed investment is likely to be a starvation proposition. Almost anyone can raise $100,000. They will set up in a garage, with the spouse keeping the books and the kids running the machines—and they will cut your prices to ribbons. If it can be done, it will be done. Count on it!

It is not just the garage-type competition you have to look out for either. A lot of fairly complex technology can be bought off the shelf on a turnkey basis. Even if a plant costs a few million dollars, that's not much of a barrier. There is a reasonable amount of that kind of money around, too. With no research and development costs, little marketing, and very low overhead, a company with purchased technology may skim off a couple of big volume contracts with low-ball bids

*M. Porter, New York: The Free Press, 1980.

and keep you scrambling to fill up your plant. A lot of commodity chemicals are in this class.

A tip-off to an easy entry business is high fragmentation—no one has more than 2 or 3 percent of the market. The reason there are so many people in the business is that it is so easy to get into and there is no particular advantage to being big. If you have any notions about going in and acquiring a whole clutch of these little guys to create a national network, be sure you know something they don't know. Clorox did it with household bleach, Lays with potato chips, McDonald's with hamburger stands—so it can be done, but be sure you do not just put a layer of overhead on what are inherently small-time operations. Take a look at this dimension before you make any more long-range plans.

The flip side of the ease of entry consideration is *difficulty of exit*. There are some businesses that are just hard to get out of. Conventional steel making is one of them. If the fixed assets are good for nothing but scrap—that is, have no market value whether they are fully depreciated or not, though they probably are—the owner will ride the prices way down below fully absorbed cost because there is no choice. You are never going to make much money competing with this company. A&P got in this bind when it found itself with a lot of money-losing stores with long leases. It lost less money keeping them open than it would have lost paying rent on closed stores. A&P is kind of an exception that proves the rule, though, because other stores did quite nicely competing with A&P when A&P was drowning in red ink. A&P just did not know how to run grocery stores—after 60 years of practice. If you have competitors who are locked in, the prognosis for profits is not good.

Bet you don't know what *oligopsony* is. Literally, it means that a few buyers control the market—and everybody knows the trouble you can get into if you private label for Sears. More generally, it means that any number of buyers control the market. Most producers of chemical intermediates are in this situation. They sell to sophisticated chemical companies that, absent a patent barrier, are quite capable of making the product themselves. As long as the supplier is willing to accept a lower return on investment than the buyer makes, the buyer is quite happy to buy in. But if the producer tries to raise his profitability above that level, the user will make it himself. There is not a very exciting future in that situation. More and more industries are becoming susceptible to buyer power as consolidation and concentration occur and know-how is diffused. Food processing may be on the verge of this situation in the United States; it has already happened in Europe.

The complement to oligopsony, of course, is *oligopoly*—a market controlled by the sellers. If you must buy from a monopoly supplier, of course you are vulnerable; but if you must buy raw materials from a competitor, you are probably also a sure loser, because the competitor will always make more money on the total transaction than you will.

If *you* are in a monopoly situation and are greedy or just inherently high cost, your days are probably numbered, too. There are undoubtedly a whole bunch of smart people out there in laboratories working feverishly to find a cheaper substitute for your product. The odds are they will find it. Phenylalanine, a raw material for aspartame, the synthetic sweetener, is in that situation. Everyone is almost certain that there must be a cheaper way to make it, and there is a big market. You can bet someone will find it. In fact, by the time you read this, someone probably will have. In more mundane cases, there may be a well-known substitute for your product, in which case the economics of that substitute will put a cap on your price and consequently your profits. Natural rubber and synthetic rubber dance around this comparative advantage tree continually. Think about it.

Contrary to popular wisdom, an industry where everybody is making lots of money is not a particularly good one to get into. It is almost certainly due for a price war—look what's happened to minicalculators and, more recently, personal computers. What you want is an industry where everyone else is hanging on by their fingernails and you are making money. They can't cut prices on you, and as long as you let them stay in business, they will hold a price umbrella over you.

Finally, there is the ever increasing possibility that your business will be legislated out of existence. The domestic sugar industry may be in that position if the borders are opened to imports. Some kinds of foundry operations may find it impossible to meet emission standards. Saccharin may be doomed as tetraethyl lead and asbestos were. Don't think it couldn't happen to you. Don't panic, but be alert and be realistic.

If you are a conglomerate, you may very well compete in several different industries and will need several industry analyses. Most companies, however, consider themselves members of a specific industry, and that is the one you should analyze. It may not be worth your while to try to do industry analyses for individual SBUs unless there is a big spread in the characteristics of the SBUs.

Once you have your market and industry facts together, you are in a position to start doing some active planning. Without those inputs you are flying blind.

For Additional Information

Ames, C. B., "Dilemma of Product/Market Management," *Harvard Business Review* (March–April 1971), pp. 66–74.

Introduces the further complication of the confrontation between the market manager and the sales and product manager.

Buaron, R., "How to Win the Market Share Game? Try Changing the Rules," *Management Review* (January 1981), pp. 8–18.

Share of what market? You decide.

Business International Corporation, One Dag Hammarksjöld Plaza, New York, N.Y. 10017.

Annually prepares five-year analyses and forecasts for most countries in the world. About $1,000 each.

Cox, W. E., *Industrial Marketing Research*. New York: John Wiley & Sons, 1979.

Finally a book on industrial market research techniques and sources. Extensive bibliographies.

Dominguez, G. S., *Product Management*. New York: AMACOM, 1971.

A good straightforward treatment of the job, given the confusion of definition.

Economist Intelligence Unit, 10 Rockefeller Plaza, New York, N.Y. 10020.

For special and periodical country surveys.

European Markets: A Guide to Company and Industry Information Sources. Washington Researchers, Washington, D.C., 1983.

Quick access to European market information.

Findex: Directory of Market Research Reports, Studies & Surveys. Find/SVP, New York, N.Y. (annual).

Just what it says it is, but almost entirely for the United States. Supplemented by The Information Catalog *(quarterly) by the same publisher.*

Garda, R. A., "How to Carve Niches for Growth in Industrial Markets," *Management Review* (August 1981), pp. 15–22.

Good information on strategic segmentation, how and why to do it.

Henderson, Bruce D., "The Application and Misapplication of the Experience Curve," *The Journal of Business Strategy,* Vol. 3, No. 3, pp. 3–9.

The originator of the experience curve explains that it does not work because everyone defines his or her own market in such a way that it is never identical to that of an individual competitor. Some good discussion of why this must be so. You can skip the last half of the article, which is a lot of arcane economic theory.

International Directory of Published Market Research. Oxford: Oxford University Press (annual).

Lists more than 8,000 studies in over 100 countries and still is not comprehensive.

Levine, S. N., ed., *Dow Jones Irwin Business and Investment Almanac.* Homewood, Ill. (annual).

A good information source.

Lubatkin, M., and Pitts, M., "PIMS: Fact or Folklore," *Journal of Business Strategy,* Vol. 13, No. 3 (Winter 1983), pp. 38–43.

An experimental confirmation of the PIMS model. Apparently, PIMS is as good as it says it is in defining "universal truths" about all business, but an industry-specific model can do even better.

Mancuso, J., ed., *Managing Technology Products.* Dedham, Mass.: Artech House, 1975.

A collection of reprints, but one of the few books devoted to marketing industrial products.

Miller, D., and Friesen, P., "Strategy-Making and Environment: The Third Link," *Strategic Management Journal*, Vol. 4 (1983), pp. 221–235.

Reports of an empirical study that shows that, among firms faced with a hostile or volatile environment, the successful ones are those that respond with increasing analytical activity. The losers tend to cut back on analysis and "do things."

Parisi, A. J., "Management: GE's Search for Synergy," *The New York Times* (April 16, 1978).

GE has dozens of SBUs, but at the top of the corporation, they deal with five business sectors.

Pope, J. L., *Practical Marketing Research* (AMACOM, 1981).

There has been a dearth of books on market research in the past 10–15 years. There has always been a lack of good ones. This one covers the ground; however, typically, there are only about two pages on anything other than consumer products.

"To Market, To Market," *Newsweek* (January 9, 1984), pp. 70–72.

Survey of companies revamping their marketing function. New York Twist Drill says sales jumped 30 percent in less than a year after formalizing marketing program. Can't promise that kind of result, but there is something in it.

5
How's Business?
Compared to What?

*This time, like all times, is a very good one if we know what to do
with it.*

—RALPH WALDO EMERSON

We will call our next set of planning sessions—which will last
two or three days—the business environment sessions. They
will turn out to be a little more than that, as you will see. At
these sessions, you will want to have all the senior executives
who will be responsible for making the eventual plan work.
This will probably include your divisional general managers—but not inevitably. It depends on how you are organized.

Some people prefer to hold their environment sessions
before the strategy/policy sessions on the principle that the
environment should guide strategy. It is a good argument,
and as usual, there is no right or wrong way. I have done it the
other way around for two reasons. First, you have been
planning for a while and the environmental analysis should
not present too many surprises. Second, if, as you review your
past planning performance in the first sessions, you decide to

change any of the basic criteria or the input procedure, you get a chance to do it right at the beginning of the cycle before anybody wastes a lot of time working under the old rules. It is a pragmatic compromise.

You are going to start your environmental analysis with the competitive environment. It can be argued that you should set the broader environmental context first in order to understand better the competitive interactions. On the other hand, one can contend that it is difficult to evaluate the broader environmental factors except in relation to the business climate you must deal with. You take the second option in order to highlight the importance of the competitive posture of the enterprise.

Get all of your top management involved in the competitive analysis. Competition is not merely a concern of the salespeople. They compete for the order, yes. But the production people and engineers are locked in a competitive struggle to get cost down. Research and development competes in product performance. The finance department competes in the terms of financing. Everyone should be aware of that competition—every day. If you are dealing with competition at the corporate level, you have only one analysis to deal with. If you decided to approach it by SBUs, you will have to allow more time.

Start with the presentation of the industry analysis if you have one. This will set the broad competitive framework that will guide you when you start setting specific objectives and strategies later in these sessions. Be sure all of the team members understand and agree on the characteristics of the industry or industries you are in.

Then get down to the specifics of the individual markets you serve. The climax of each market analysis will be the estimate of the distribution of sales among the various suppliers serving the specified market—the shares of market (SOMs)—and the estimated shifts among those SOMs.

Next put your team to work. Let them cross-examine the analyst and make the analyst earn his or her credibility. The whole team has "gotta believe." If differences of opinions cannot be resolved, you will have to tentatively accept the analyst's figures and ask for further confirmation.

Now let's see what the team can collectively contribute to

your understanding of the competitive profile. First agree on the five or six most important competitive factors in your business—the considerations that have the greatest influence in determining whether a buyer will choose one supplier over another. In my first book to make things easier I specified the competitive characteristics to be used. Now you are certainly able to set your own.

What about price? In some commodity-type products and even some services, price is irrelevant because everyone charges about the same. At the other end of the spectrum, in luxury products or industrial products that constitute a small part of the buyers' total cost, price may be equally irrelevant. Quality or service may be the overriding consideration in your market. If it is, the vendor who can command the highest price has the competitive advantage. All other things being equal, that vendor has more money to spend on advertising and promotion, and can afford to build better quality into the product. This vendor can also provide better service. And if worse comes to worst, the vendor can always cut the price. The supplier who has to sell at the lowest price has no place to go. That company has no competitive options.

The cost of producing a product or service is almost always a competitive factor, but not invariably. In certain fashion and recreation businesses, it doesn't much matter. If it is important for you, look at it "at the factory gate," because it is the more or less discretionary money between manufacturing cost and sales revenue that permits the development of competitive clout. If you think that in your industry there is a wide variation among competitors in the percentage of indirect cost, overhead, do an additional ranking on the basis of net margins. It is always possible that those heavily burdened companies will get their acts together and squeeze out some of that overhead. More likely, when the going gets tough, they will decide to take some marginal business and ignore those allocated costs.

The quality of a product or service is usually a competitive factor, but again not always. If everyone is selling to set specifications, quality may drop out of the equation. What is quality in carbon steel plate? Then there are some markets where no one will pay for quality and it becomes irrelevant.

Service can be a big competitive factor, but it can mean a

lot of different things. You may have more than one service dimension. Or you may have none. If you are a parts supplier to a Japanese automobile maker who practices "just-in-time" inventory control, split-second delivery service is a must. In certain production equipment industries, 24-hour spare parts delivery or field repair service is the whole game. If the customer's plant is shut down with a broken machine, it must be fixed *fast*, and nothing else really matters. Technical service—holding the customers' hands until they learn how to use your product, solving their problems for them—may be critical to compete in some businesses. Be careful of this one, though. Times change. In the early days of an industry, technical service may be the determining factor. But as customers get more sophisticated or develop their own technical staffs, it can lose its significance. An extensive technical service organization—no matter how good and how highly respected in the industry—may become an unwarranted tax on net margins. If the competitor whom you rank as having the best service organization is losing market share, you might reasonably infer that the customers are not buying service.

Physical distribution—having field warehouses all over the country or a big fleet of company trucks—may give a supplier a significant advantage, particularly with a lot of cash-short customers who do not like to carry inventory. Then again, it may just be an unjustifiable expense.

The quantity or quality, or both, of a distributor network or of field sales offices is a strong competitive factor in some industries. On the other hand, if products are sold mostly on national contracts, it means nothing.

Sales effectiveness—the ability of the sales force to get an order—may be a determining factor. So might marketing effectiveness—the quality of advertising and promotional campaigns, the ability to introduce new products successfully.

In some consumer products, design capability may make or break a company. In high-tech industries, it is often the innovative quality of the research department or of engineering.

And then there is financial strength. In some industries,

this may not be important, but in rapidly growing markets where technology is changing rapidly, it can be the determining factor. In a classical shake-out, it is almost always what determines who gets shook. Think about this one very carefully. Are there people out there who could, if they wanted to, buy up market share, raise the ante on production technology, lead into financial depths where you would have difficulty following? Watch them very carefully, and try to guess what is going on in their planning sessions. In contrast, are there competitors who are so thinly financed that they cannot afford the investment to keep up with the growth of the market? There might be some way you could preempt their share of the growth.

The possible list of competitive factors is long. Don't try to list all the competitive considerations in your industry. The sales and marketing people will have to be sensitive to them all, but for strategic purposes, pick out the four or five or six really pivotal ones. Put these competitive factors across the top of a chalkboard and list the principal competitors, including yourself down the side (see Figure 3). Note the functional competitors from your market analysis at the bottom, just so you won't forget them. Now under each factor, *rank* the suppliers according to their relative strengths—No. 1 being the supplier with the best competitive situation. Don't try to *rate* them on a scale of one to ten. You will get into a lot of unnecessary discussion, and it will not really tell you anything much. What you are interested in is who is better than who. What if the group does not agree among themselves? That tells you one thing. Information about your competition is either inadequate, or it is not uniformly disseminated among your managers. For the present, you will have to force a rough consensus and resolve to find out just what the facts are. Maybe assign the dissenter, if there is an outstanding one, to look into it.

When you get the numbers all laid out, step back and see what you've wrought. If all the competitors are ranked about the same on one factor, that tells you it is not really a competitive factor and maybe you should pick another one. If you have a competitor who has poor quality, no service, a lousy sales force, the lowest prices, and an increasing market

Figure 3. Form for analyzing competition.

COMPETITION

SBU _____ Market Size $ _____ Growth Rate _____ %/yr.

Rank competitors relatively on each factor, with (1) the most favorable and (10) the least.

	% Market	$(\uparrow \downarrow \leftrightarrow)$[1]	Manufacturing Cost[2]	Pricing[3]	Quality	Service
1.						
2.						
3.						
4.						
5.						
6.						
7.						
8.						
9.						
10.						

[1] $\uparrow$ = gaining share, $\downarrow$ = losing share, $\leftrightarrow$ = holding.
[2] Relative cost of factors of production. This would be operating cost in a service company.
[3] The highest price is the most favorable in this context.

Functional Competitors

	Total Sales	Growth (%/yr.)
1.		
2.		
3.		

share, you people are in a price market. Or at least there is a substantial number of price buyers out there. The flip side of that is the competitor with acknowledged quality, good service, great research and development, and a decreasing market share; this also suggests something about the market: It just will not pay for quality.

See if you can see any correlations. Are there any factors that all the people who are gaining share seem to be good at? Or where all the suppliers who are losing share are deficient? How do you stand on the factors that are really important to the market? If you have all threes and fours across the board, you are going to have trouble getting out of the "also present" category. If, on the other hand, you have mostly ones and twos and one six, you know where your shoring up must be done.

As you look at this competitive analysis, remember that these are the people you are going to have to make it against. When you start putting your marketing plan together—if you aspire to increase sales at greater than the market growth rate you have up there at the top of the sheet—you are saying you are going to pick up market share. Whom are you going to take it away from? There are only 100 points to go around. As a general principle, you do not want to go after the winners— the ones who are gaining market share. They are doing something right—or at least trying hard. It might be worth your while, though, to try to figure out what the gainers are doing that makes them so good. They may just be buying market, but then again they may be smart.

It will be awkward to try to make substantial gains out of the hides of the 1 and 2 percenters. There is just not that much there to take: They offer a scattered target, and the chances are that they have some more or less captive business that they get because of propinquity, personal relationships, or special service. It may not be very gentlemanly, but your most fruitful targets are likely to be the competitors who are losing share, whether they are doing it consciously or not. Ideally, you look for a stumbling giant, but the fates are not always so kind as to provide one. Your next best shot is to look for dimensions in which you are strong against the major competitor's weakness. It could be in marketing, service, or quality. Or maybe you should consider cutting prices. In any case, concentrate your artillery at one point on the line.

In the less likely case that you have decided that this is not such a hot market anyhow and you are willing to relinquish share, you can see where to cut. It is no use having the best technical service in the industry if you are not trying to further your market penetration. Maybe you should raise prices. Maybe you should use your hotshot salespeople somewhere that they can make you some real money.

There are lots of sophisticated or at least more complicated systems for analyzing competition. Some companies keep comprehensive data banks on all competitors and virtually try to psychoanalyze them from a distance. This is what used to be more commonly called "commercial intelligence" and is much more studiously practiced outside the United States than it is here. But it is impressive what you can learn by organizing what you do know about your competitors in as simple a format as is described here. If you do not even have enough information to fill out the simple matrix shown in Figure 3, you are playing blind man's bluff and you might as well try baccarat.

General Environmental Analysis

Now let's look at the broader environment. You really should take one day a year to consider the external circumstances under which your industry operates. If you do not set aside special time for it, you just won't do it. An outside speaker to break up your habitual thought patterns is a good idea, although they have gotten more expensive than they used to be.

One thing you are going to have to do at this session is agree on the rate(s) of inflation you are going to assume for the planning period. If you do your projections in current dollars, you will have to know it in order to know what the numbers mean. Even if you plan in constant dollars, you will have to assume some inflation rate to make your cash flow forecast. You should also state some kind of assumption about the real growth in gross national product over the planning period. You may also wish to make some umbrella assumptions on interest rates, labor rates, energy costs, and other general parameters of the business. These assumptions will be distributed to all people involved in developing plans to be sure they all work under the same assumptions. That is one of the primary reasons for recording assumptions: to assure that everyone is calculating from the same bases.

Maybe you have already set up an organized environmental scanning operation. If you are sensitive to energy prices or are a multinational or are in any aspect of the sweetener business, you have had ample demonstration of how important it can be and how few people do it well. If you have set up such a function, you are already well beyond the scope of this book. If you have not, you might at least step up your information inputs. Of course, you read the trade literature and get some guidance from your trade association. But there are other published sources. For multinationals, there are now a number of country survey services available. The oldest are the ones done by the Economist Intelligence Unit; the British have been at this for a long time. Business International in the United States provides services, and so do the international banks.

There are all sorts of tip-sheet newsletters out of Washington. They are not always right, of course, but in general they are quite knowledgeable even if they cannot be fully clairvoyant. In these days of government regulation—and deregulation—you need all the clues you can get. Most of the big banks, including the Federal Reserve Banks, have economic publications that are quite good, and they are free. *American Demographics* is good for sociological trends, and so is the British journal *The Economist*, even for the United States.

I know you have too much to read now. But you had better broaden your scope, even if you have to thin it out a little bit. You can maybe spread the load around among the top managers, but be sure they understand their responsibility to circulate pertinent information among their colleagues. If you have a top-notch information specialist or librarian, you may entrust him or her to scan certain publications and put out an abstract letter periodically. This is risky, though, because no matter how professionally competent such a person is, inevitably he or she will not be fully aware of all the strategically sensitive concerns of the company. You have to make a conscious effort to avoid being a "heads down manager." Build some kind of discipline into your planning process to force yourself to stop and look around you every so often.

It is true, as Robert Louis Stevenson said, that "the world is so full of a number of things," but unfortunately it is only in nursery rhymes that this assures us "we should all be as happy as kings." But come to think of it, who said kings or shahs are always happy?

If you are not using the format I provided in my earlier book (see Figure 4), I recommend it to you. It looks formidable, I admit, but it really is not that hard to use and it forces people to crystallize their thinking and saves a lot of rambling discourse. By now your key people should have achieved some sort of comfort level in preparing themselves for planning meetings, so ask them to get their thoughts together and fill out their forms (except for the last four columns) before you meet. As a kind of prod, ask each member of your team to analyze at least one factor in each of the areas of technology, economics, government, and social change.

Merge the environmental worksheets from all the members of the planning team (this could be done in advance of the meeting). The next step is to come to an agreement on the assumptions you will use in making your plans. Assumptions are not simple forecasts. They are based on two factors: probability and exposure. If an event is highly probable but really would not have a large impact on your company's business, you may be safe in assuming it will not happen. On the other hand, an environmental development that would open up a huge opportunity for you may warrant an assumption that it will come to pass, even if the odds are less than even. You cannot afford to miss this opportunity if it should present itself. The form is intended to quantify your assessment of exposure and probability and thus direct you to the appropriate response. Obviously, the numbers are not intended to be taken too literally. They are order of magnitude categories.

Figure 4.   Sample environmental analysis—1985.

Environmental Event	EXPOSURE			Earliest Possible Year	PROBABILITY					50/50 year	Company Response Time, Yrs.	Watch	Investigate	Contingency Plan	Action Plan
	10% Next Year	50% in 5 Years	100% in 10 Years		10%	30%	50%	70%	90%						
A	+				X							J.Doe	M. Roe	?	
B	-	-				X									Smith
C	+							X							
D		-		1987						1988	1				
E		-		1986						1988	2	L.Brown	K.Jones		
F		+		1987						1987	3			?	
G			+	1987						1989	4				Douglas
H			-	1988						1990	3			L. Lewis	Curtis

+ = opportunity   - = threat

In the example in Figure 4, Events A, B, and C are the short-fuse items. Event A is low probability and low exposure so you will take the risk and act on the assumption it will not happen. B is marginal, but you may have a little lead time. You cannot afford to ignore it, though, so have someone check it out and then make your assumptions. C has better than even odds, and the opportunity is sufficiently attractive for you to act on the assumption that it will happen.

Events D, E, and F could have a major impact on your affairs, but you have a little time. D will probably happen within four years, but it will not happen next year, and you could adjust for it with one year's warning. You do not have to do anything about it yet, but you should keep an eye on it since it will be very harmful when it happens. You do not think E is likely to happen in less than three years either, but it could happen as early as next year and could do as much harm as D. Furthermore, it will take you two years to eliminate your exposure. This is a very hazardous position, and you had better have somebody find out exactly what is going on as soon as possible. F represents a big potential opportunity, and the chances are that it will materialize within a couple of years. Even if you start immediately, you might not be able to get in position in time to exploit it; but you cannot start any sooner and are unwilling to chance missing the opportunity, so you will go on the assumption that the event will occur and you set up an action plan right away. G would be a real windfall in the long haul. It too could occur before you could get ready for it, but it probably won't. You want to get started positioning yourself to take advantage of the possibility, but your action plan will probably proceed at a fairly deliberate pace. H could put you out of business entirely, and it could arrive right about at your response horizon, but you really don't think it will. You had better be ready, though, just in case, so work out a contingency plan and keep it on the shelf.

Agree on the proper categories for your environmental factors. Ask someone to keep an eye on those that you have assumed you can safely ignore to be sure you were not unjustifiably sanguine. For the iffy ones, ask someone to investigate and make a recommendation as to what the proper course should be. Set a due date commensurate with the urgency you think the situation warrants. In the cases where you agree the situation is serious but not imminent, ask someone to block out a contingency plan to be available for the next planning cycle, at which time you will reevaluate your assumption. For those events that you agree you must assume impact on the company within a time frame that requires more or less immediate action, assign an executive to prepare an action plan proposal to be considered at the next series of planning sessions.

The cases where you have assumed a substantial unfavorable impact within the actionable period of the plan are the most important. These are the threats from the external environment that you must position yourself to counteract. These threats are potentially the most dangerous problems a management faces, and they are the ones most often overlooked or ignored. They are often subtle and likely to arise in a sector of society that is unfamiliar to the endangered management. It is not your familiar competitor who is likely to do you in. It is some guy you never met from another industry who comes up with the radical new technology or the innovative marketing approach who will pull the rug out from under you. Or some bureaucrat. Or a change in life-styles. Don't get blind-sided. Look around. And then scramble if you must.

The external events that could cause a major increase in your business potential are commonly called opportunities. And so they are. If you think you see one, take a shot at it as soon as possible. Do something! Probe. Experiment. If you think you cannot afford to divert major resources to these possibilities, try a little bit. Get your feet wet. It may be all an illusion anyhow, and at least you won't feel guilty about what might have been. If your reconnaissance proves favorable, you can probably dredge up some more resources somewhere to get in a little deeper. Just don't sit around and talk about it.

Key Result Objectives

Although we have called this a business environment meeting, we are going to go one step beyond just analyzing the environment. This is the time to set your corporate key result objectives (KROs).* Set your KROs now because you do not want to set them by extrapolating your past performance. They should be based on the business environment in which you operate and how good you think you are compared to the competition. You may have done it differently in the past when you started planning, but now with some practice under your belt you should be able to set KROs realistically against the opportunities presented without getting carried off into flights of fancy.

Sales Growth

The first KRO you should set is almost certainly growth in sales volume, partly because it is the easiest to do and partly because the other KROs will tend to be derived from it. In some industries, you will have to do it in physical volume because of erratic prices, but most likely you will do it in dollar terms. I recommend you set all your objectives in *current* dollars—that is, the kind that will actually appear on your eventual operating statements. You could set your objectives in *constant* dollars and avoid dealing with the inflationary effect, but that really only accommodates one of the factors and I think it is easier to use explicit assumptions and then make adjustments. And you are going to have to work in current dollars anyhow to make a cash flow forecast. However, if you work in current dollars and inflate your sales revenue, be sure you also inflate all your costs accordingly or you will get very unreal margins.

If you do it right and build up your sales objectives from GNP, inflation rate, industry and market growth, and competitive performance, you can make adjustments every year

*Called "primary objectives" in my earlier book. The nomenclature has been changed because "key result objectives" is more descriptive and is somewhat more common usage. Furthermore, you can have key result objectives at any level of responsibility, and I avoid the complication of trying to explain that the senior executive's secondary objectives become his or her subordinates' primary objectives.

by comparing reality with assumptions and find out whether or not you are actually accomplishing what you set out to do. If you get it all on a computer, it's a snap.

You and your planning committee assumed some rate of growth for the general economy—the GNP. You also agreed on some inflation rate. From your market data, you should know whether your industry or your market tends to grow faster or slower than the general economy and by how much. That gives you par for the course. Then look at your competitive position and agree how well you should be able to do compared to the potential. That is your sales growth objective. Presumably, you will not settle for less than average performance. If you have to admit you are outclassed, you should change your environment, change the nature of your business, change your mission. If you think you are better than the other guys, by how much? Before you answer that, consider the amount of growth in the market you will have to capture if you want to increase your market share.

In Figure 5, we have assumed that your market is growing at 12 percent per year. Suppose you want to grow at 15 percent to double your volume in five years. How possible

Figure 5. *Relationship between market growth and sales growth.*

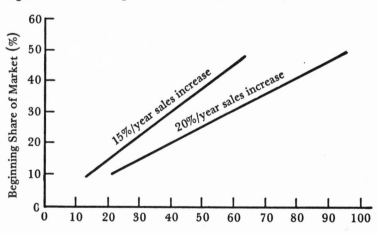

Percentage of Market Growth That a Company
Must Capture if Market Is Growing at 12% per Year

this is depends in part on how much of the market you start with. If you have a modest 10 percent of the market, you could achieve the 15 percent growth rate by merely capturing about 13 percent of the new business and you would gain a modest one and one-half share points over the five-year period. However, if you begin with 50 percent of the market, you would have to capture two-thirds of the new business and increase your market penetration to 57 percent by the end of a five-year period. Particularly note that, if you already have 50 percent of a market growing at 12 percent a year, you would have to capture virtually *all* the growth in the market in order to increase your sales by 20 percent a year. Come on! Be reasonable. That is just not going to happen. You had better go back and broaden your mission to open up some new potential if you want that sort of growth.

The sales growth objective particularly is set almost entirely on the basis of external—exogenous, if you want to be fancy—factors. How good are you, compared to what?

Write a short paragraph explaining the strategy behind your sales growth objective: Where will the major push be? Where will you slack off or withdraw? What will be your pricing policy, your competitive posture, and so on? Don't make a long essay out of it; just hit the high points. It is mostly to serve as a reminder of what you were thinking when you set the objective. It is a good idea to record the major assumptions behind the objective at the same time: "We will attain this objective, assuming . . ." certain price and cost actions, technological developments, competitive actions and reactions, government actions or lack thereof—whatever conditions you want to impose on your commitment to achieve this result. Do this for each of your KROs as you set them. In fact, you should do it for any objective at whatever level.

Earnings Growth

Your next KRO is growth in earnings. You set it by a similar process. How are your current earnings? How do you view your posture during the coming planning period? Have your earnings in recent years been essentially flat in spite of increased sales? Are you in a "we gotta do better!" mood? Then your earnings growth rate will have to be greater than your sales growth, which is another way of saying your net margins on average must be increased. Or are you entering an expansionist, development phase in which you will sacrifice current earnings for rapid growth? Then your earnings will increase less rapidly than your sales revenue. You would reach the same conclusion if you decide that you must reorient the business and enter a number of new business areas because of unfavorable trends in your present business. Overall sales growth might not be spectacular, but earnings growth is likely to be even less so. Matched growth rates of sales and earnings define a "steady as she goes" posture of balanced development.

Check your margin performance against companies comparable to yours. The Department of Commerce issues averages for some industries. Look in *Forbes* or *Fortune* or in your trade press. Get other people's annual reports or, better yet, their 10Ks. Now, where do you think you should fit compared to those guys?

Profitability

Let's put the third leg on the stool. The return on resources objective, even more than the sales objective, is the one most clearly determined by considerations outside of the company itself. It is the universal standard by which all economic activities are ultimately measured and the one by which your management performance can be judged against all other managers in the world. You know what your cost of borrowing is. You can easily find out the average return on investment (ROI) in your industry, and most likely you know what ROI your leading competitor achieves. Given your resources in plant, people, technology, and market position, how well should you be able to perform? Obviously, you have to do better than the aftertax cost of borrowed money. Should you do as well as the industry average? Better? Or maybe, quite simply, what return will the board of directors accept?

Or you can force return on assets (ROA) objectives from your intended rate of sales growth by the formula:

$$\% \text{ ROA} = \frac{(\% \text{ sales growth per year}) \times (\text{equity/total assets}) \times 100}{\% \text{ earning retained}}$$

If you do not change your debt/equity ratio or your dividend policy, your sales growth rate aspirations determine the ROA that you must achieve. More practically, of course, it works the other way around. The ROA you achieve determines how fast you can grow unless you are willing to increase your debt leverage or cut back on your dividend payout or both.

Your profitability objective is going to be the toughest one to achieve. When you put your final plan together, it will be the last one you calculate for the simple reason it is the consequence of all your management decisions and is truly the bottom line. Theoretically, at least, you should be able to do all the other wonderful things in your plan if you could throw infinite resources at them. (I say, theoretically, because the government does not seem to make it work out that way.) But you do not have infinite resources. In fact, some of the resources you have you probably borrowed. The bankers will take their return on those assets before anyone else gets anything.

This is where acquisitions present a problem. You can buy earnings all right through an acquisition. But if you must pay 20 times earnings for it, which is not a bad price for a reasonably good company, that is only 5 percent ROA. That is less than the aftertax effect of prime rate borrowings (in 1983). You would have to have other assets equal to the purchase price earning 3 times that much to average out to a barely tolerable 10 percent return. If you are going to buy growth through acquisitions, you had better have some fancy notions about what you are going to do with the acquired company to boost its earnings—fast.

So, set a profitability objective that you feel represents an acceptable standard for your stewardship of the company's assets. Technically, that is a little more complicated than it might seem at first glance. Just how and where are you going to measure it? The simplest formula to use is:

$$\frac{\text{Net income after taxes}}{\text{Book value of total assets}}$$

That is the ROA that is used in the growth formula given above. You need only two numbers: the bottom line on the balance sheet and the bottom line on the profit and loss statement. The rationale is straightforward. You get your assets from a lot of sources. Some you own, some you borrow, some you get for nothing (accruals and accounts payable). Your job is to make money with those assets, and the more you make the better. You have a number of costs of doing business, among which is paying interest.

There are a lot of objections to this procedure, but there are a lot of objections to every other way of measuring profitability, too. Most of them arise from the use of the book value of assets. Fixed assets that are depreciated to zero but are still in use obviously constitute a resource but do not appear in the equation. Goodwill arising from an acquisition represents a real investment, but what happens as you write it off? People do a lot of cobbling trying to make the formula more realistic. They subtract payables from assets because they are free assets. Yes, but so what? They are real and you use them. Some people add accumulated depreciation back into the asset base to get gross fixed assets to avoid the automatic escalation of profitability that results from depreciating assets.

It has become increasingly common in recent years to add interest to profit to get the numerator of the ratio. The economics of this is beyond argument. Interest is unquestionably a return paid on assets employed. When interest is added back in, it is common to use "invested capital" (equity plus long-term debt) as the denominator on the principle that these are the true "investments" that deserve a return. "Interest" then usually means only long-term interest. Short-term interest is taken as an expense. This kind of calculation, though, could show a return on investment when the company is operating at a loss as long as the interest payments exceeded the amount of the loss. Somehow that does not seem right in the practical world.

There are other permutations, but when you get through all the hairsplitting, a plain net profit return on total utilized assets may be as meaningful as any of them. Add the interest back in if it makes you feel more righteous. It will make the return percentages look better, particularly if you are highly leveraged. One thing you want to be particularly careful about is comparing your profitability to any kind of industry averages or making intercompany comparisons; be sure you know what formula is being used. *Forbes* and *Fortune,* for example, use different methods to calculate profitability.

There is another complication coming down the road. Auditors and the securities commissions are becoming increasingly insistent that leased assets be capitalized. This is to counteract the abuses of off-balance sheet financing. It means that you must calculate the cost of a leased asset and show it as such on the balance sheet, with the rent payment obligations as a liability. Of course, this increases your asset base. Then you include rent as part of the realized return, and the top of the fraction is profit plus interest plus rent. I do not suggest that you set your profitability objectives in these terms just yet, but you should be aware that we might be heading in that direction.

What about return on equity (ROE)? It is still quite commonly used. In any company more than a few years old, it takes the one figure on the balance sheet that bears no relationship to any kind of objective reality and divides it into the net profit. Equity, or net worth, does not represent what the owners have invested. What they have invested is what they paid for the stock or, more rigorously, what they could sell the stock for today. Net worth is not what the company could be sold for. Look at acquisition transactions. Prices paid bear no detectable relationship to the "book value" of the companies. Equity, or net worth, is an accounting accident. Nobody knows what ROE means, except in a brand new company.

Development Objectives

The three sets of objectives we have established are what might be called health and welfare objectives. They set the conditions necessary to keep in good shape for the next several years, but they do not really say where you are going. There should be things you want to accomplish for the future development of the enterprise over and above just staying healthy. If you have not been setting any key development objectives, it is reasonable to assume that you have not been doing much for the long-term development of the company. You have been fine-tuning and expanding the businesses you are in but not really taking on anything new. This is a very hazardous posture to be in. At the minimum, you run the risk of eventually running out of steam. Quite likely your relative competitiveness will deteriorate—look what happened to the automobile companies. If you are underspending on research and development or on market development, your reported profits are fictitious. You are actually slowly liquidating the company.

Now you are really on the spot to do some strategic thinking. Where do you really want to go? Even if nobody on your team has a convincing grand passion about a specific development project, force yourselves to set at least one development objective. It will create some excitement anyhow.

"This is the time that we are really going to develop our export sales or upgrade our export markets to offshore production."

"The major project for this planning period is to weed our product lines, get rid of the dogs that are going no place, and get out of the businesses where we have no future."

"We must get into a position where some significant part of our earnings is not subject to the swings of the construction industry."

"We must get better control of our raw material sources (backward integrate?)."

"We have to clean up our balance sheet."

Pick one and make it *the* major campaign. Force yourselves to look at the long-term future of the company, because if you don't, nobody will. Do something in this planning period that will make the next planning period easier and more successful.

These development projects are going to cost money—probably both expense and investment money. They will make your other key result objectives harder to attain. They may not contribute significant sales or earnings during this planning period, but they must be done to maintain the momentum of the company.

Reprise

All right, where are you? You have agreed on what you are and where you are. You have blocked out a scheme of where you think you ought to go. Now you have to fill in the details to see if it all makes sense. If you want to take this first cut to your board before you go on with the detail work, it is not a bad idea. In multidivisional companies, the divisional managers often must make a presentation to the corporate executive group at this stage to get concurrence before they proceed to prepare their formal plan. This is often called a "strategy" presentation, which is what it is—the broad outlines of the opportunities and the approach. The rest is "tactics".

SBU Plans

Your tactical units are your SBUs. You will want a separate plan for each of them. That is why you set them up. Depending on how big you are and how you are organized, that may mean a separate planning team for each SBU. Or it may mean that the same group of functional vice-presidents will have to take them up one at a time. In either case, the planning team will want to consult with a lot of other people in the organization and maybe outside as well. This is where you broaden your participation.

You have set the broad strategy for the corporation in your first two sessions. The mission or charter of each SBU was agreed upon. Market information has been assembled and confirmed. Environmental situations that impact a single SBU have been identified and a specific response indicated. Viewed as a separate business, what can each unit expect to accomplish?

The SBU teams will set their own KROs—sales, earnings, profitability, and one or more development objectives. They must all use the same GNP and inflation assumptions, or you can't add the numbers together. Otherwise, SBU objectives and corporate objectives should be done independently of one another. The one should not dictate to the other—either way. You want to see as realistically as possible just what contribution each SBU can make to accomplishing the corporation's KROs—no more, no less. The SBU KROs will be scattered above and below the corporate KROs. You hope the pluses and minuses will more or less balance out, but most of all you want to know just where that balance is.

The sales objectives come first. They must be compatible with the competitive situation and the business environment. The SBU teams may want to harden up some of that environmental information, particularly the competitive information, before they go on the line with specific sales objectives. Fine! That is both their privilege and their responsibility. They know they will be held accountable.

Each SBU's earnings prospects, like the overall corporation's, will depend on whether it is in a development phase, a hold-the-line phase, or a withdrawal cashing-in phase. However, when you quantify the earnings objectives for SBUs, there is no point in going beyond the "contribution to profit and overhead" line because nothing that happens beyond that point relates to a specific SBU. It does mean, though, that you should take marketing, distribution, and appropriate research and development expenses above that line, even if your normal operating statement practice is to absorb them in corporate expense. I know some of you will say that you cannot allocate these expenses to SBUs reasonably—and maybe you can't—but I will bet you could if you tried, and you might learn some interesting things about your business.

Each SBU will have a capital budget that may or may not reflect a facilities plan, and from this and the earnings objective, you can calculate the expected profitability. If that comes out unacceptably low, the SBU had better come up with some cost-savings projects to improve earnings or some asset recovery ideas to cut down on the required investment.

Remember, too, that each SBU will show a return on assets at the "contribution" level, and that must be considerably higher than the corporate ROA.

Unless an SBU is in a hold-the-line posture, it needs some development objectives. If it is in a "milking," withdrawal position, these objectives will have negative values, but there should be some specific plans for the extent and pace of withdrawal that is intended.

OK! Turn your SBU teams loose. Tell them you want their plans back in about ten weeks. In a large organization, you may have to give them more time. The degree of detail you require is a matter of management style. You may ask for detailed marketing plans or facility plans for each SBU if you think it is warranted. But the heart of the plan will be the objective structure, and you want that to be complete and solid.

Do not ask for detailed action plans at this stage. You are going to have to see the overall pattern of the SBU and development objectives before you can approve any of them, and there is no point in doing all the detail work before the go-ahead is given.

Development Planning Task Force

Assigning the task of planning strategies for meeting the corporate development objectives may present some problems. If such an objective represents an entirely new kind of business venture, you will have to empanel some kind of task force. The initial step is to designate a planning team to get the necessary information together and to lay out a proposal for implementation. Doing this will take some time, and the members of the planning team must be relieved of some of their regular duties if they are going to do a good job of it. Since you have said that the long-term future of the company depends in substantial measure on attaining this objective, you very much want them to do a good job. Their proposal will contain recommendations for staffing. Conceivably, the planning team or some part of it could become the implementation task force that would be assigned full time to making it happen. Probably more likely, the first action in the plan will be to put somebody in charge of the program. If the objective is to develop the export market, for instance, the first step is to appoint an export sales manager. He or she can be reassigned from inside the organization, or a specialist can be recruited from the outside.

In either case, good planning practice—good management practice—dictates that the person who is going to implement the plan be party to its architecture. This is awkward, but it cannot be helped. Your planning task force can detail the situation, suggest the objectives, and estimate the approximate cost, but there is no point in its working up a complete strategy because that is the prerogative of the person who assumes the responsibility for the objective.

It will be very handy, though, when you go looking for your "export manager" to have the situation analysis and objectives, and even the expected costs, as a kind of job specification. You can tell the candidate exactly what he or she is expected to accomplish.

If a development objective clearly pertains to an existing SBU, even though it is outside of the present strategy of that SBU, you have a bit of a dilemma. Your first instinct will be to delegate responsibility for the objective to the person responsible for that SBU, particularly if that person is a product or a division manager. However, you are counting on that person to keep the basic business of the SBU thriving. He or she would have to work on the special development Saturdays and Sundays. Or maybe the person would get so intrigued with it that the regular business would suffer. Something has to give. You can't pour a quart into a pint jar. On the other hand, if you give the responsibility to a specially assigned person, you are likely to have a morale problem. The SBU manager may feel a lack of confidence, or may just resent being excluded from the fun. The specially assigned person may have difficulty grafting onto the regular line organization. You will have the same problem if the development objective is in a functional unit, say introducing automation into the plant or a new major research field into the research department. There is really no good answer to this problem. You are much more likely to get satisfactory results from a specially assigned honcho or task force, but you may pay a price.

If you can possibly muster the human resources, set up task forces to pursue the development objectives. Some companies call them new venture teams or new business teams. Of course, if you are big enough to have a business development department, this is its job. A line executive in an SBU that is not doing much exciting might take on a second hat as the head of such a venture team. Just be sure this person does not drop the bone he or she has for the prospects of the one in the water.

What you want first from the development planning task force is an assessment of the prospect and a proposal for how to approach it. Let the task force do a quick situation analysis, confirm the reasonableness of the objective (or recommend its adjustment or rejection), and decide the general outline of an approach, with estimates of time and cost requirements. You will consider these analyses and recommendations along with the SBU plans and make the final decision about organization and staffing. If you accept the proposal at that time, you will put the objective in your plan and provide for the approximate cost, but you will have to wait, probably for many months, before you know exactly how this one is going to be done. Patience!

Administrative Plan

There is one other piece that should be assigned at this time—the administrative plan. Somebody has to look ahead for all those staff departments. These units probably will not affect strategy much, although conceivably strategy could affect them if the demands for certain kinds of services will be increased substantially. However, you must have the numbers to plug into your final financial forecasts, and they might as well be based on some kind of reality rather than on just a percentage of something or other. What about office space? What about a new computer? If you are going to expand the personnel function or institute central quality assurance, they must be accounted for someplace. Some of your action plans to correct weaknesses may come in here.

What about the planning department? A cynic might suggest that one of the reasons administrative plans are often not done very rigorously is because they usually include the planning function. Be that as it may, put somebody on the job. Do you think that administrative costs will stay constant while sales increase 50 percent? Don't you believe it! But you say you'll be able to spread overheads over a larger volume? Maybe, but get the numbers. Those kinds of economies of scale usually prove particularly elusive. If your overheads have been trending up as a percentage of sales or earnings, you need a good strong positive plan to get them under control.

While the SBU, development, and administrative plans are being put together, you will want to have another session to examine the trends of your organization's operational dynamics to see if you can spot any strategic weaknesses or strengths that should be factored into your long-range plans. The amount of time you allocate for this session depends on several things. First, how much operating detail do you want to consider? That, too, is a matter of style. You might do it in a couple of hours. However, if you want presentations by your human resources person, your comptroller, your vice-president of research, and so on, you will need more time. You should also invite all the participants to submit items for the agenda, situations that they view either with alarm or with great expectations. If you get a lot of agenda items, you had better figure on at least three days to discuss them.

Who should those participants be? It could be your whole planning team. On the other hand, a good case may be made for restricting the group to corporate executives—staff people, if you will. The line people have their hands full putting together SBU plans. And there is also the possibility that one of them might be responsible for one of the strategic weaknesses.

Holding your operations analysis meetings separate from your other planning meetings is somewhat unorthodox, but it serves to give some protection against extrapolative-type thinking. More about all this in the next chapter.

For Additional Information

Ansoff, I. H., *Strategic Management.* New York: John Wiley & Sons, 1979.

A rather complex attempt to relate management decision making to environmental and internal cultural factors. Kind of heavy going, but you might find it thought-provoking.

Leontrades, M., *Strategies for Diversification and Change.* Boston: Little Brown & Company, 1980, Chap. 6.

Deals with the effect of planning on organizational structure and the trend toward business segmentation. Some data.

Pierce, J. A., II, and Robinson, R. B., Jr., "Environmental Forecasting: Key to Strategic Management," *Business* (July–September 1983), pp. 3–11.

A rundown on environmental scanning. Lists a lot of sources, and the bibliography will lead you to more. Not comprehensive by any means.

Porter, M., *Competitive Strategy.* New York: The Free Press, 1980.

A definitive treatment of all aspects of competitive analysis, and its use in setting strategy. It is doubtful that any company will adopt Porter's total procedure as proposed, but seeing the whole picture laid out in a rational pattern is worthwhile anyway. Part II deals individually with specific kinds of competitive environments. Appendix B gives rather simplistic directions for an industry analysis, but it is a place to start.

Robinson, S. J. Q., "What Growth Rate Can You Achieve?" *Long Range Planning,* Vol. 12 (August 1979), pp. 7–12.

If you are into equations, here is a bunch of them. The most important says, ". . . the maximum growth rate that can be financed by a business by total reinvestment of net income is equal to its internal rate of return."

Smith, S., III, and Walsh, J. E., Jr., *Strategies in Business.* New York: John Wiley & Sons, 1978.

Offers a good action-oriented form for dealing with environmental events on p. 77. Interesting thing about this book: It devotes almost half of its pages to developing information inputs for planning strategy. The clue is that Smith's title at Monsanto was "Information and Planning Director."

6
Know Thyself

Most ailing organizations have developed a functional blindness to their own defects. They are not suffering because they cannot solve their problems, but because they cannot see their problems.

—JOHN GARDNER

I cannot say I completely agree with John Gardner's statement quoted above. I encounter a great many organizations that recognize their problems but do not do anything about them. One of the functions of a formal planning procedure is to identify and quantify critical strategic weaknesses and place them before the senior management in an explicit form. There is an implied assumption behind the process that, once the management is presented with these problems in such a structured context and acknowledges their importance, the managers' sense of responsibility and self-respect will prevent them from pushing the problem back under the carpet. It turns out that this assumption is somewhat naive.

We are not talking about Mr. Gardner's kind of problems—the ones that are consciously or subconsciously submerged. We will get to those later. Nor are we concerned with the suddenly explosive crisis. Managers who panic in a crisis usually do not last long—at least not in industries where crises occur with any regularity. Most managers are only too ready to jump into harness when the fire bell rings. It may sometimes be rather painful to see a CEO who spent his or her middle-management years in the finance department undertake to personally straighten out the production mess at the Des Moines plant, or to have the group vice-president with the engineering background tackle the exodus of the key sales managers in the western region, but at least they are doing something. It is the structural, the positional problems that are allowed to persist year after year, even after they have been formally acknowledged.

Operational Analysis

Most strategic weaknesses do not arise full grown from the sea but develop over a period of years. If that is true, could they have been anticipated and perhaps avoided? Quite likely so.

However, when things are going to hell—not in a handbasket, but slowly and quietly—you are not likely to spot the problem from a monthly operating statement. Again the question is: "Compared to what?" Compared to what it used to be. It is the trends that are unfavorable, not necessarily any one particular datum. In order to have trends, you must have numbers over a period of time. How long a period of time? The statisticians have all sorts of formulae to determine how many points are required to determine a statistically significant trend. As a practical matter, though, you may have a shutter somewhere in the past that limits how far back you can go: the time you changed your fiscal year or your accounting system, or made a major integration step. Barring such a limitation, the rule of thumb is: Go back as far as you are going to go forward. If you are making a five-year plan, take five years of history and current year estimated and project for five years. There is no particular theoretical rigor to this practice, but it seems to work out pretty well.

Why fork over all this history? "Trend is not destiny." Agreed. "You cannot plan looking into a rearview mirror." Not if you never turn around and look ahead. But there is a kind of Newtonian law of time series data that says a trend in motion will continue in the same direction until acted upon by an outside force. If the trend is unfavorable, you want that outside force to be you.

What kind of trends are you looking for? Almost all will be in ratios, because ratios will pretty much cancel out the effects of inflation and the change in size of the enterprise. There are, of course, an infinitude of ratios that you could watch, and you can make up a better list of the ones that are significant in your business than I can prescribe from some kind of general theory. However, there are some pretty basic ones.

We have already talked about share of market, which is the ratio of your sales to your industry's sales. If it is going up, you are developing your position and possibly can justify some depression of profits because you are buying market share. If your market share is dropping, you are literally liquidating an asset of the company and you had better be getting a good price for it in the form of enhanced profits.

Return on investment is another ratio: that between profits and the dollar-denominated resources committed to the enterprise and measured in one of a number of ways. If this ratio is going down, you are buying profits by pouring more capital in, just as you might buy sales by cutting prices. Unless, of course, your net margin is shrinking. Net margin— the ratio of profit to sales—is something you probably do watch. It is a good operating indicator, but for strategic purposes, it can be misleading. What makes a good net margin differs from industry to industry. One percent is great in retail groceries but would be a disaster in fine chemicals. It depends on the investment involved. It is highly probable that the same net margin is not equally good for all your SBUs. It is possible that, if you sell some plant and buy components, you could have a lower net margin and be better off. If you do any vertical integrating, your net margin has to go up to justify the additional investment. The only question is, how much? If you watch this trend, be sure you know what is actually happening.

Gross margin, the ratio between sales minus manufacturing cost and sales, is another standard. A low gross margin business in general has fewer strategic options. It handles a lot of money but does not have much choice about what to do with it. If your gross margins are sliding, even if the net is holding up, you may be getting squeezed into a strategic corner. If you have a raw material with a highly volatile price because it is publicly traded or if you process raw materials with wide differences in cost, such as alloy steel and titanium, your gross margin percentage may not be very meaningful. It can vary widely while the net stays solid as a rock.

There are a lot of other things you might look at:

- Labor costs as a percentage of sales for one. Labor rates tend to rise faster than the rate of inflation and, if that percentage is crawling up, you are becoming more labor intensive and you may be in for a cost/price squeeze unless you plan your way out of it. This was a large part of A&P's problem.
- Marketing cost as a percentage of sales. In some industries this is almost trivial; in others it is pivotal. If your marketing costs are rising, does it really mean that the industry is becoming more marketing intensive or do you have a cost control problem?
- Research and development as a percentage of sales. Are you buying present profits by selling off the future of the company?
- Average size of order. Is your market concentrating or dispersing?
- And, of course, such factors as inventories, working capital, and administrative overhead.

Below is a list of suggested ratios for operational analysis, but it is by no means comprehensive:

Turnover or Efficiency Ratios

$$\frac{\text{Net sales}}{\text{Long-term debt} + \text{preferred stock} + \text{common equity}}$$

$$\frac{\text{Net sales}}{\text{Receivables}}$$

$$\frac{\text{Net sales}}{\text{Inventory}}$$

$$\frac{\text{Sales}}{\text{Net working capital}} \quad \text{defined} \quad \frac{\text{Net sales}}{\text{Current assets} - \text{current liabilities}}$$
$$\text{as}$$

$$\frac{\text{Sales}}{\text{Gross working capital}}$$

$$\frac{\text{Sales}}{\text{Net fixed assets}}$$

$$\frac{\text{Sales}}{\text{Gross fixed assets}}$$

$$\frac{\text{Sales}}{\text{Total net assets}}$$

Profit Margins and Rates of Return

Operating Income as Percentage of Sales:

$$\frac{\text{Operating income}}{\text{Net sales}}$$

Pretax Earnings as Percentage of Sales:

$$\frac{\text{Net income} + \text{income taxes}}{\text{Net sales}}$$

Posttax Earnings as Percentage of Sales:

$$\frac{\text{Net income}}{\text{Net sales}}$$

Operating Income as Percentage of Gross Fixed Assets:

$$\frac{\text{Operating income}}{\text{Gross fixed assets}}$$

Return on Owner's Equity:

$$\frac{\text{Net income}}{\text{Net worth} - \text{intangibles}}$$

Decision Ratios

Quick Ratio:

$$\frac{\text{Cash and equivalents + receivables}}{\text{Current liabilities}}$$

Current Ratio:

$$\frac{\text{Current assets}}{\text{Current liabilities}}$$

Criteria of Financial Soundness

Debt/Equity Ratio:

$$\frac{\text{Long-term debt}}{\text{Owner's equity}}$$

Depreciation as Percentage of Net Fixed Assets:

$$\frac{\text{Depreciation and amortization}}{\text{Net fixed assets}}$$

Capital Expenditures as Percentage of Retained Cash Flow:

$$\frac{\text{Capital expenditures}}{\text{Available for common + depreciation} - \text{common dividends}}$$

Other General Ratios

Fringe Benefits per Employee:

$$\frac{\text{Total fringe benefits}}{\text{Number of employees}}$$

Direct Costs per Employee:

$$\frac{\text{Cost of goods sold}}{\text{Total number of employees}}$$

Direct Costs per Production Worker:

$$\frac{\text{Costs of goods sold}}{\text{Number of production employees}}$$

Indirect Cost per Employee:

$$\frac{\text{Sales and administrative costs}}{\text{Total number of employees}}$$

Direct Cost per Labor Hour:

$$\frac{\text{Cost of goods sold}}{\text{Total hours worked by all employees}}$$

Direct Cost per Production Worker Hour:

$$\frac{\text{Cost of goods sold}}{\text{Total production hours worked}}$$

Raw Materials Used per Labor Hour:

$$\frac{\text{Raw materials used}}{\text{Total production hours worked}}$$

Raw Materials per Dollar of Plant and Equipment:

$$\frac{\text{Raw materials used}}{\text{Plant and equipment} - \text{depreciation}}$$

Inventory per Dollar of Sales:

$$\frac{\text{Inventory}}{\text{Net sales}}$$

Accounts Receivables per Dollar of Sales:

$$\frac{\text{Accounts receivables}}{\text{Net sales}}$$

The point to remember is that you are looking for trends that will clue you into changes in the nature of the business. Computerized information systems make it only too easy to crank out reams of spread sheets. Don't get carried away. You do not need to follow these things month to month. But as you go into the early phases of your planning cycle, pick out a few parameters that your gut tells you have been shifting over the years and have one of your number crunchers check them out and see where the trend will take you in five years. It may not be significant. Then again it could be quite unacceptable, and you had better start doing something about it.

The computers do solve one problem. It used to be a very tedious process to generate a valid trend line through a set of historical numbers. You had to hire a statistician to do it. Now you can get one from many hand calculators. There is really no excuse for dodging the issue. If you do not know how to do it, ask some high school kids. They likely can show you how.

You know, of course, that any specific year's value is going to deviate to some degree from the trend line. A mathematical colleague or maybe your computer manual will tell you, on the basis of the scatter of your historical data, how wide these deviations are likely to be in a specific case so you can have a plus or minus figure for your forecast. That can be a shocker, too. If the values are swinging too widely, you may be vulnerable to perturbations that you could not survive and then you have a serious control problem. On the other hand, it may mean that your performance is so erratic, possibly for reasons beyond your control, that the trend line is just not very meaningful.

Do as much of this kind of operational analysis as you have time and patience for. The actual calculations, of course, will be done in advance of the meeting. Let your controller make a presentation. Maybe also your human resources person or your production manager or your chief engineer. Some charts help a lot.

If you do not get any surprises from your operational analysis, fine. If you spot trends that are going seriously against you, put them at the top of your list of strategic weaknesses that you are going to do something about.

Strategic Weaknesses

You asked your people to submit items for the agenda to be considered as strategic weaknesses. If you have been having planning sessions for five years or so, you should not need the crutch of a form such as was provided in my previous book. Your top people should be able to recognize a strategic weakness when they see one—situations that seriously impair the company's ability to pursue its chosen strategy and that literally threaten the health of the enterprise. The lists should be very nearly identical. If there are significant divergences, the first order of business is to deal with the strays and agree as to whether or not they belong on the list.

If when you consolidate the lists you end up with a couple dozen items, your company sounds like a basket case. More likely, though, you are probably just worriers. No matter. The only practical tactic is to pick out three or four or maybe five items to be given the crash treatment in the coming planning period. The rest have to be tabled for consideration the next year or delegated down through the regular line organization for the best treatment those people can give them.

Now let's look at that short list. Are any of the strategic weaknesses that you listed in your first plan five years ago still on the current list? What about the ones from last year? There should not be any from five years ago and the ones from last year should at least be well on their way to solution. We defined *solution* in this case, you will remember, as being brought to a condition you can live with but that probably still needs considerable improvement.

If you have permitted some of the problems to drag on, you know you will have trouble meeting your objectives because that is how you defined the problem in the first place. You will have to devise a procedure for nailing these items to the church door and not letting them get out of sight until some effective action has been taken. Without getting philosophical, much less psychoanalytical about it, the practical fact is that most managements need all the procedural stiffening they can devise to assure that really fundamental problems are addressed.

A company management knows that its market has become much more sophisticated and, although it has good, seasoned salespeople, it has nothing that by any stretch of definition could be called a marketing function. The company is constantly being outflanked by the competition. Somebody suggests that they should at least hire a market research analyst but, since there is uncertainty about just where he or she would report, nothing is done about it.

The new product development process is a zoo. Either there are so many projects that none of them ever seems to get ready for test market, or people are sitting around tinkering with very long-odds possibilities that no one is really enthusiastic about. Successful product introduction record is abysmal. An interdepartmental new product committee is empanelled, meets once or twice, and evanesces.

Nobody really likes to tackle serious problems. You make yourself unpopular. There is seldom any glory in it. You do not produce any startling new initiatives. Usually, the best you can hope for is to achieve some sort of tolerable "normality." And yet the job must be done, or all the grandiose schemes will come to naught.

Correcting Weaknesses

If you have this situation well in hand you can skip the next couple of pages. For the rest of you, let's see whether we can generate some diagnostics. There are some fairly common symptoms that suggest the cause of the lack of action.

First, have you been setting the fox to catch the chicken thieves? I recommend that you not assign responsibility for correcting a weakness to the person who has nominal responsibility for the function in which the weakness exists. I know this is hard advice to follow. In a small company, there are not likely to be any spare managers around for such an assignment. No matter what the size of the company, problems of personalities, egos, and authorities always arise. But you say the problem threatens the vitality of the entire enterprise. If it were easy, it would not be serious. This is a job for a task force or a temporary assignment. Making it temporary provides the added advantage that, if eggs have to be broken the scrambler does not have to live with the bruised scramblees. The logic is irrefutable. The incumbent executive either does not see the problem, does not understand the problem, does not know how to solve the problem, or is afraid to solve the problem. If this were not so, the problem would not exist. Some kind of new broom must be introduced.

What if the primary responsibility for the situation lies with the CEO? This can happen, for instance, when the weakness arises from disheveled organization structure that just cannot get things done. The basic situation is the same. If the CEO knew a better way to organize things, he or she presumably would do it that way. If the CEO has sufficient wisdom and courage, he or she will admit needing outside help. The CEO could, of course, bring in an organizational consultant. However, the company might be equally well served if the CEO appointed a task force of senior executives—who probably, subtly or not, brought up the question in the first place—to come up with an alternate organizational design. This has the additional advantage that, if the CEO accepts the design, the members of the task force have the implicit obligation to make it work.

Which indirectly leads to some observations about the nature of task forces. There is a good deal of literature on task force management—some of it good—so we will not go into the technicalities here. The point to get clearly in mind is that a task force is not a steering committee. A task force is an action unit with power and authority to act. Ideally, it should be a full-time, although temporary, job. If that is completely impracticable, the members must still expect to make a substantial time commitment to the task. They are expected to *do* things, not just talk about them. This means they must relinquish some or all of their usual duties by delegation to subordinates or by arrangement with their peers. If there is no such delegation of responsibility, the task will not get done. All this applies equally to any individual who is assigned a project to correct a weakness.

The necessity of assigning special responsibility for a project to correct a weakness leads to the second diagnostic. Did you create a sense of urgency? Making a special assignment to an individual or task force is the best kind of objective evidence that the management is convinced the problem is important and urgent. Making it clear that the assignment is temporary, even if the time span is not specified, reinforces this sense of urgency. The delegee is not expected to make a career out of it. If this person is flattered but not entirely delighted with the assignment, that may be all to the good because he or she will introduce his or her own urgency from a desire to get back to more enjoyable work. Some of the companies that regularly use task force "repair crews" are suspected of intentionally choosing members who are disgruntled with the assignment on the theory that they will get the job done and get out in the shortest possible time. Obviously, if you are going to do that, you must be able to rely on the responsibility and competence of your people or you will get a slapdash job.

There are other things you can do to keep people's attention focused. I recommend that, if you assign a project director who is not a member of the planning team, you contact this person immediately and ask him or her to come out to the meeting place. That is mostly for show, but it will get the designee's attention. You can set up a performance incentive. The CEO can request a personal verbal report weekly or monthly. You can require a monthly progress report to the board of directors. It does not matter whether the directors read it or not. The image is created. Sometimes a kind of public tally board is effective. Use your imagination.

Now the third diagnostic. You did set up an action plan, and it didn't correct the problem. Everybody got discouraged and gave up. What do you think you are? Omniscient? So you made a mistake. Sometimes you almost have to "make a mistake" in these situations. If the problem is lack of new products and the research department swears it has all kinds of new product possibilities in its notebooks but nobody ever listens to them, you are almost forced to set up an action plan to mine that vein before you try something else. Set up a firm timetable, though, and if you do not have much confidence in the possibilities, you might start blocking out a backup plan, but you must give the first plan a try. If your problem is deteriorating quality and manufacturing is adamant that it is a machine problem or a training problem, you pretty much have to go along with this diagnosis to a point. If you try to go to an independent quality assurance function directly, it is going to be very difficult to make it work. Sometimes patience is the only counsel, but keep up the pressure.

The fourth diagnostic: Are you setting proper objectives to correct weaknesses? This is such a basic precept of planning that I hesitate to mention it. However, it does tangle up efforts to correct weaknesses. The first thing to remember is that you are not striving for perfection. All you have to do immediately is improve things to a tolerable degree. There is a tendency to overshoot. The basic difficulty is to determine what is tolerable, what is an acceptable objective. You know you have a problem. You know it is hurting you badly. But just how deep is the problem? If it is a runaway cost factor, you have it in numbers. You know how much it is costing you. With a little effort you probably can find out what the average experience for that factor is in your industry or at least in a few comparable operations. Then you can aim for parity. If the competition is clobbering you in the Northeast, you can set up a crash program to reclaim 10 percent of the market in that area.

But what if the problem is lack of new products? You can set an objective to have one successful new product introduction a year and then quantify successful. Or you can shoot for 10 percent of total sales revenue from new products in five years. This may require an explicit definition of *new product*, but that can be done. These objectives reflect what you are actually trying to accomplish. The trouble is they are fairly long range. You will not know for years whether your approach has been successful.

Sometimes you have to treat symptoms. Does your new product problem arise because of a paucity of new ideas, or are you working on so many ideas that the system is overloaded? Are you pursuing too many concepts that prove to have little commercial promise or flogging old projects that have been around for years? Thomas Peters in "The Mythology of Innovation, or a Skunksworks Tale" says that if you do not have a preliminary design in 30 days, a prototype in 30 days, and field test data within a year, you should drop the project because you are just fiddling with it. Maybe you need tighter scheduling. Maybe it is better screening that is required. Maybe it is new sources. You can set operational objectives on the premise that they address the problem. That

means you have to be sure you understand the problem—
dissect it, get to the root of it.

If you do that, sometimes you will find that you got the
problem wrong. What you wrote down as a "lack of adequate
delegation and clear lines of authority" may actually be a
counterproductive selection and promotion policy or a failure
in training and development. "Lack of adequate vertical
communications and consequent poor morale" may turn out
to be the consequence of fuzzy direction and the absence of
coherent objectives. The communications channels may be
all right; it may be the message that is at fault.

If you cannot see your way clear to final elimination of a
weakness, take it a bite at a time. Take an action that you
think will improve the situation. If you are not sure what
action to take, try something. If that does not help, try
something else. But do something. Do not let the situation
fester and generate nothing more than a lot of lengthy discussions that add up to the conclusion: "Ain't it awful?"

Setting objectives to correct weaknesses is not always
easy. That is why they are so often muffed. Correcting strategic weaknesses is not easy. That is why they are so often
permitted to persist. In no other phase of the planning process will you encounter the need for change in such a naked
form. And in no other phase of the planning process will you
encounter the natural human resistance to change in such
glorious profusion. Weaknesses occasionally arise because of
a gross shift in the environment or a spectacular move by a
competitor, but most frequently they result from an accretion
of poor practices in the past. The enemy is in fact us, and in
any action to correct weaknesses, there is usually an implied
criticism of somebody, past or present. Recognize, therefore,
that making this aspect of planning work will require more
organizational discipline and more intellectual honesty than
any other part of the process. It requires very careful definition and very rigorous controls to bring this part of a plan to
fruition.

Once you have identified a weakness, assign a task force
leader immediately. Ask him or her to submit in four weeks,
sooner if that is practical, a detailed action plan proposal to

correct the weakness. Create that sense of urgency. Agree on who will approve the proposal for implementation, and get the action started. Don't wait for any other phase of the planning process to catch it. Then track progress at the very highest level of management. There is nothing more important—although there may be many things more pleasant.

Corporate Strengths

Once you have dealt with your weaknesses, you can consider your corporate strengths. After five years, you should have pretty well worked over any obvious stray strengths that were lying around. If you kidded yourself about their commercial value, you have long since been disabused. Your relatively favorable positions in the industry should have been documented in your competitive analysis. New opportunities arising from developments outside your industry should have been revealed in your environmental analysis. You should no longer have to go through the formal rigmarole to document your strengths that you did five years ago. The only factor you might be missing is the opportunity to package up something you do now in a different way for a different market, possibly even for a different use.

The most obvious options are to literally repackage. If you make industrial products, you could put out a consumer-size pack. If you sell to consumers, you could back up into institutional sizes. If you are packing gallons of olive oil for the ethnic food market, you could pack some four-ounce bottles as a beauty aid. You have probably already thought about this and either are doing it or have decided that the content of the package is irrelevant in your case and the differences in marketing would put you into a new kind of business that you know nothing about.

Opportunities in horizontal line extensions are not always so obvious. If you are not already doing it, you are probably overdue for some sales analysis. With data processing systems, it often requires little effort, although it is shocking how often these fancy systems are incapable of producing any information in useful form. If the Pareto Principle operates in your enterprise, as it does in most, about 20 percent of your customers will provide 80 percent of your business. In any case, concentrate on the major customers who provide the bulk of your sales. Don't bother with the "twelfth of a dozen, assorted" types. What do these key customers have in common? Are they big or small? Manufacturers or fabricators? Furniture makers or food processors? What? If you sell entirely to grocery stores, then what kind of grocery store shoppers buy your products and would recognize your trademark? You may come up with more than one major category. Within each category, then, what do these people *all* buy that you do not sell them? There is your candidate list. Go down the list and see if there are any of those items that you could make, or arrange to make, or have made for you. These are customers you know and who know you. You will still have to compete with other suppliers, but at least you can get in the door.

If you are in industrial products, you will get another benefit out of such a sales analysis. By categorizing your customers, you will identify the nature of *their* customers. It is sometimes easier to track your customers' customers than it is the people you deal with directly. If you know your customer sells mostly to the automotive, the construction, or the garment industry, you do not have to depend on what his purchasing agent tells you; you can get projections for those markets directly. Or if you really want to know what is going on, you can sometimes go to your customers' customers directly and ask them. Chances are they will be more honest with you than they would be with their own suppliers.

I mentioned in my earlier book the possibility of exploiting exceptional service capabilities outside the company. In these days of rapid growth in the service industries, this is always worth looking at—particularly since service activities usually require relatively little capital investment. This kind of opportunity usually arises fortuitously. A company seldom builds up a great industrial hygiene department with the intention of peddling it commercially. If they have one, though—partly because they were lucky with people—they might well consider the possibility. The big question is: Is it to be a nice little source of side income for the department, or is it to be a significant part of the corporate strategy? If it is the latter, it means that the basic nature of the enterprise will shift. Selling services is different from selling stuff.

One company packaged up its expertise in designing and administering employee benefit programs and offered it as a service to other medium-sized companies. It makes a nice little earnings flywheel for their highly cyclical machinery business. But it did not fit in the hardware culture of the organizing company and was spun off as a separate subsidiary.

But we are still talking about more or less logical extensions of what you have been doing—what is increasingly called "linear thinking" or, more physiologically, "left-hemisphere thinking." What about the really innovative insight, the flash of genius, the kind of thinking that put 3M into the sticky buck slip business? It is all well and good for me to talk about "outside-in planning" and "looking at yourself through the eyes of potential customers," but how do you actually do it? How do you get people, including yourself, to think imaginatively?

A lot depends on how you think about brainstorming, about the whole tribe of creativity workshops that have been hawked around the business community for about 20 years now. I won't comment one way or the other about the merits of some of the more complicated techniques, but there is one little exercise they do at MIT that you might try at one of your planning sessions.

At MIT, the class is asked to list all the possible things that can be done with a common lead pencil. What you should do is pick one of your products or product groups and ask everybody to list everything that could conceivably be done with that product. Disregard cost, the volume of use, the availability of alternate devices, and all other practical considerations. It will loosen people up. It will probably be good for a couple of laughs. You might just possibly, perhaps by the combination of a couple of crazy ideas, come up with something that is worth looking into. But do not take the exercise too seriously because that will suppress the very kind of freewheeling, free association you are trying to encourage. People should understand it for what it is: a demonstration of just how wide ranging thinking can be if you let it run loose. If this sort of thing seems fruitful, you might consider looking into one of the "creativity gurus."

Obviously, I do not know any magic formula for getting people to think creatively. If I did, I would set up shop as a guru myself. But there are a few basic rules. Don't be too critical when ideas are still in the embryonic state. Let them develop a little before you put them through a screen. Try to find a way to keep a lid on the person on your team who is always sure "it will never work." There is always one. Set up a think tank or a "skunk works" where the wild-eyed visionaries can get a little insulation from the everyday world before they expose their brain children to chilling reality. Reward innovative ideas, particularly psychologically, even the ones that get rejected. I know one company that ran a competition among the middle managers for the most original strategic idea. There was a panel of judges and the prize was a two-week, all-expense-paid vacation for two in Hawaii. Just like a sales incentive contest. They did not have to wait for the proposal to work out; the idea itself had to be exciting. This certainly is the direct approach to the problem. I cannot say that the contest came up with any world-beating ideas, but it did get people's attention, and at least indirectly some of the suggestions were useful.

Probably the most important thing about building on corporate strengths, just as with correcting weaknesses, is that, if you get an idea that seems to have promise, don't let it lie around neglected. "Someday we should look into . . ." "I bet we could . . ." "What ever happened to that program to . . .?" These are some of the saddest words to hear around the top management suite. They are sure to sour the spirit and squelch innovative initiatives. If an idea seems to have some merit, put somebody on it—somebody who is enthusiastic about it and is likely to become a "champion." Let this person get the facts together, assess the potentials and the probabilities, and bring in a proposal at the next planning meeting. But keep the person on a rather short leash. Don't let the idea be studied to death. Check it out in the market at the earliest possible time. If you can, plan to cobble up some kind of jerry-rigged prototype right away. Go talk to a couple of potential users. They may help you finish the design. Then, if it will not fly, hit it in the head and get it off the agenda. Don't get caught agonizing over what might have been. Above all, do not waste your time making long, self-congratulatory lists of all the things you do well. So you have the best-run mailroom in the industry. You can't build a strategy on that!

The cost and consequences of the action plans you approve to correct weaknesses will ultimately be folded into individual SBU plans or into the administrative plan. Proposals to exploit strengths will be held in abeyance until you see how the whole pattern works out.

For Additional Information

Kastens, M. L., *Redefining the Manager's Job*. New York: AMA-COM, 1980, Chap. 14.

More on the uses of task forces.

Peters, T. J., "The Mythology of Innovation, or a Skunksworks Tale," *The Stanford Magazine* (Summer 1983), pp. 13–21; (Fall 1983), pp. 10–19.

The co-author of In Search of Excellence *makes a strong case for small task forces (fewer than seven members) with maximum freedom to get things done. "Most invention comes from the 'wrong' person in the 'wrong' place in the 'wrong' industry at the 'wrong' time."*

7
Speaking Objectively

My object all sublime I will achieve in time.

—W. S. GILBERT

Setting good objectives is not only the key to good planning, it is the essence of any planning worth the name. You have set up key result objectives. If you are like most human beings, when you plot the historical trend line and then the projected objective line, there is an upward bend at the "now" point. That bend may be pretty acute. This is vulgarly called a "hockey stick" or "dog leg" and often elicits some cynical snickers. There *should* be a kink in that curve. You are planning to do some new things, to make some changes, and that should have some effect on the trend. However, remember, the trend already may reflect new products, marketing campaigns, price actions, and other initiatives in the past. You must do some new *kinds* of things to make that curve bend. Doing more of what you have been doing in the past will only keep you on the trend line. If the break in the curve is very slight, it would indicate that you have been exploiting the potential of your situation fairly thoroughly. You do not need to make many changes. Just keep up the good work—unless, of course, you want to escalate your aspirations and put yourself in a new situation—but maybe the challenge is just

111

to maintain the pace you have established. If the "hockey stick" is acute, you have a lot of work to do.

Plot your objective line from the last year on the trend line for which you have real historical numbers. That is probably not the actual figure for the last year. If you were planning in 1982, your actual figure was probably well below the trend. You had to depend on the inevitable effect of economic recovery to bounce you back up onto the historical trend, and then you had to grow from there.

Rubbing Against Reality

When you set corporate KROs, you were establishing an hypothesis. Then you sent out your SBU leaders to test that hypothesis against some possibly ugly facts. (If you didn't segment your business, you set out to test the hypothesis yourself.) If the organization is of any size, your SBU leaders will have to go down to the guys in the trenches—who will have to make it happen—to see if they think you are living in a dream world. Then you want them to come back with their best analysis and recommendation to confirm, modify, or reject the objective hypothesis.

Can you assume that after several years of practice you can count on your people to do their homework, to come to the next meeting with their stuff together? If you still must do all the inventing and designing around the planning table, you probably will never get it all done. What you need is a well-thought-out proposal that you can question, criticize, modify, accept, or reject. If you are not getting that kind of input, it may be that there is some more cosseting required, but it is at least as likely that you are just not demanding it. Adjourn a couple of meetings and say you will reconvene them when there is something concrete to discuss, and most people will get the picture pretty quickly.

Even if your people have gotten pretty skillful, you might begin to impose a general format on them. What you want are these basic concepts:

Situation	Strategy
Objective	Cost

That applies no matter what function the plan addresses. In fact, that is the gross outline of your total plan, too. And you want numbers—good numbers—but you do not want them all up in the body of the proposal. Put the documentation in attachments.

First, the *situation:* the history, the trends, the ratios, the technology, and so on. This section can be augmented by as many exhibits as the proposer deems appropriate. You will want to know particularly what the competition is doing, what the government is doing or is likely to do, and possibly some socioeconomic considerations.

Second, the *objective:* "Given all of the above, we should reasonably expect to be able to do so-and-so." If the logic will not hold up to this point, you can drop it all right here.

If it sounds reasonable so far, you can proceed to the *strategy:* "This is how we propose to go about it."

Finally, there are the resources required: the *cost* in capital, expense, human resources, elapsed time. The objective divided by the resources required gives you what is commonly called a cost/benefit analysis even though the ratio is actually inverted.

You can do this all on a few sheets of typescript if you are willing to take a lot of numbers on faith. Procter & Gamble does it on a single page, but every number is absolutely reliable—and they know they can count on it. You can demand more highly documented proposals, but in that case, keep the logical sequence: "This is the situation that provides us a certain opportunity if we do certain things at this estimated cost."

Marketing Plan

Your first key result objective, sales growth, will be achieved through your marketing plans. You will want a marketing plan for each of your SBUs. These may all be done by one senior marketing/sales executive, by product line managers, by division heads—whatever your organization dictates—but they should each be signed by one person, not a department or a committee, because this is the person who will be responsible for achieving that SBU's sales objectives.

The marketing plan itself should not be more than four or five pages, but it can have all the data attachments wanted. The *situation section* should contain the important conclusions of the market analysis—the trends in usage, price activity, new applications, growth trends, and so on. It should confirm and expand upon the competitive analysis done earlier. What are the competitors doing? What are they likely to do? Where are prices going and why? Are there likely to be technical developments? New products? New competitors? New marketing tactics? Whatever is pertinent in determining market strategy.

Whether it says so explicitly or implicitly, the *objective section* starts, "Therefore, given this situation, we should be able to achieve the following." The objectives may contain some exceptions and conditions: "We can make the five-year objective, but we are going to be slow getting started in the first two years." Or "The third year will be a bad one because one market segment is pinching out and we cannot replace all that business immediately." Or "We must have a product with thus and so performance characteristics within two years, or we will be massacred." Or whatever. Remember, too, that the market plan need not necessarily anticipate growth. It may outline an orderly withdrawal or a holding pattern.

The *strategy section* then says this is how we are going to do it. There are lots of ways to lay out a marketing strategy, but the two-by-two matrix shown in Figure 6 is probably as useful as any. If you are statistically inclined, you can generate the prospects in Quadrant 1 by extrapolating your past sales trend. These are the sales to kinds of customers you currently have, with the kinds of products you presently make, in the areas you currently sell. This is your baseline. You can also generate it by forecasting the trends in your customers' businesses and your share of the market. The difference between that baseline and the objective you have set for yourself is the "planning gap." The gap fillers will have to come out of Quadrants 2 and 3 and possibly 4. Quadrant 4 is usually beyond the charter of an SBU, but if the SBU is based upon a production technique or a certain raw material, it is certainly a place to look. Quadrant 2 may involve going

Figure 6. *Two-by-two matrix for marketing strategy.*

	Old Markets	New Markets
Old Products	1 Sales Development	2 Market Development
New Products	3 Product Development	4 Business Development

into new sections of the country or additional countries of the world. It may also involve finding new applications for your existing products or invading price strata where you presently do not compete. Quadrant 3 is essentially horizontal integration. What else can you sell to your present customers? You do not necessarily have to develop them yourself. You can act as a reseller. Or you may be able to buy a product line without buying a company.

Do not include the effects of a key development objective program (corporate KRO) in the SBU marketing plan even if it clearly falls within the purview of the SBU. By definition, the purpose of the development objective is not to create short-term sales or earnings, and including its results, either positive or negative, will obscure the plans for the ongoing business.

If you like graphics, Figure 7 is a kind of all-purpose form for displaying the segmentation of objectives. You can see that it can be easily extended either horizontally or vertically to provide any number of boxes you want. Here it is used to summarize the objectives and strategies of a marketing plan. The annual SBU A sales objectives are broken down into five subobjectives. Note that rows 1 and 2 are Quadrant 1, "Exports" are Quadrant 2, "Improved C-Widgets" are Quadrant 3, and "New Products" are Quadrants 3 or 4.

The marketing plan ends with the *cost section*. This is essentially a marketing expense budget. It should include a human resources budget and any capital or expense charges entailed in opening new offices, distribution centers, or other activities associated with marketing. Do not expect your marketing people to include product cost or any allocations in their plan. The one exception is product development costs, and that depends on how your operating accounts are set up. If the product development department is part of marketing, the costs should be included here. If it is part of research and development, the costs will appear there; but they really should be identified as chargeable to a specific SBU.

At the end of the marketing plan—or maybe even better, at the beginning—should be a very careful statement of the assumptions on which it is based: steady real prices, all cost increases passed along in total through price increases, no price war (inflation rate assumption is set by the corporation); no unfavorable actions by FDA; no radically new product introductions by competitors. Whatever. Don't make assumptions about ability to produce or develop new products or to obtain financing or anything else that is within the capacity of the company to accomplish. Those are objectives, in other parts of the organization admittedly, but they must be accepted by appropriate people before the marketing plan is approved.

The Production/Facilities Plan

After a lapse of at least 20 years—maybe since the big production push, cost-be-damned days of World War II—people are once more beginning to realize that plants not only must make products but also must make profits. Productivity does count, and quality performance, too. Your earnings performance is going to be the difference between the sales revenue that the marketing plan has assured you and the production costs plus overheads. Production costs have to come from the production people. They are going to have to take those volumes from the sales objectives and estimate what the labor, materials, and conversion are going to cost to make all

Figure 7. Form for summarizing the objectives and strategies of a marketing plan.

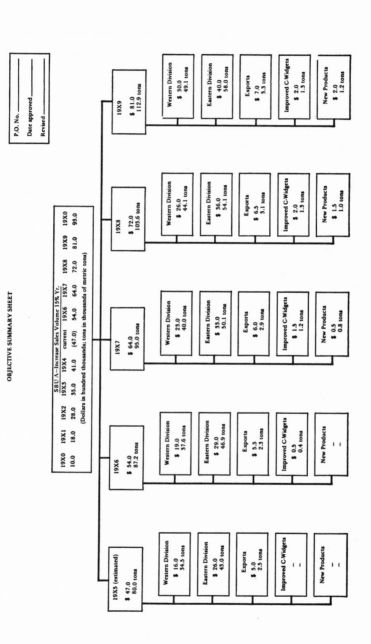

those products. In order to do that, they are going to go back to the marketing people and say they need to know more about the product mix, the seasonality of sales, the geographical distribution of sales, and a lot of other stuff. Marketing will say they cannot tell production all that because they don't know. So what else is new? Marketing and production people are always fighting anyway.

Actually, if they sit down with their respective records, they can come pretty close. Nobody expects them to be perfect, and production will build in a cushion anyhow. Seasonality can be calculated statistically. It is not when the peaks occur that is important but what their amplitudes are. Product mixes do not change arbitrarily and usually not suddenly. Historical trends should be pretty reliable, particularly when adjusted for information from the market analysis. The market analysis combined with the sales analysis should provide a pretty good grip on the geography of sales.

See if you cannot get your production people to build up their cost objectives from the costs of factors of production and from a calculation of fixed and variable costs. There will be a tendency to use traditional percentage margins and a qualitative reassurance that unit costs will go down as volume goes up. Actually, engineers like to massage numbers, and, if you get them involved, they can be quite enthusiastic. The trouble is that too frequently in the past the production people have been excluded from or have absented themselves from the planning process because nobody listened to them anyhow. That is a risky practice these days. Get your manufacturing vice-president thoroughly into the act. Stroke him or her a little. He or she sat through all that marketing talk.

Did some of your weaknesses involve production costs? Be sure the cost savings that the action plan promises are factored in here. You are going to get them, aren't you? Does production have any cost-savings projects of their own? Are there going to be any new cost items to meet Environmental Protection Agency or Occupational Safety and Health Administration requirements?

The production/facilities plan should be presented in the same format as any other plan, one for each SBU. In the *situation* section, present plant capabilities, percentage of capacity used, trends in the costs of the factors of production, technological developments, labor availability and productivity, whatever is important.

The *objectives* should answer such questions as: What can be done to increase productivity? What are the effects of increased utilization of capacity? What can be expected from changes in processes, packaging, scheduling? Get some numbers here—not lots of them but the important ones. As has so often been said, the process of forcing the production people to think through what actually is out there to be accomplished is as important as actually writing it down in the plan. But sometimes you have to make them write it down in order to get them to think it through.

The *strategy* section will address these questions: How will the plants be scheduled? What cost-savings programs are proposed to be effective when? Where will new equipment be installed and when?

The production people may wish to break down their subobjectives within an SBU differently from what was done in the marketing plan—that is, instead of sales regions, new products, new markets, and so on, they may find it more meaningful to do it by plant or by department. There is no harm in that. It is a good idea for them to project their present cost structure as a baseline and then show cost-savings projects as separate subobjectives with a negative cost number. What you want is the manufacturing cost and consequent earnings figure up there in that SBU-by-year box. The cost characteristics of the new products group within an SBU will obviously have to be design estimates.

Before your production people hit you up for new capacity, see that they do an analysis like the one in Figure 8. There is more about this in my first book.

If you set your SBU earnings objectives at the "contribution" level, the production people can just subtract their manufacturing cost objectives from the sales objectives and get contribution figures by SBU by year. Then the accounting department can apply the appropriate allocations to the yearly totals and get a profit before tax figure for each year. If actual earnings objectives will be set for each SBU, then the accountants will have to apply overhead factors to each SBU to bring down an earnings figure. If you are real elegant, you may use different factors for different SBUs, particularly

Figure 8. Model production-unit capacity analysis.

Critical Points	Units	Manufacturing Costs Fixed	Manufacturing Costs Variable Unit	Manufacturing Costs Total	Marketing Costs	Average per Unit Manufacturing Cost	Average per Unit Contribution	Marginal Unit Cost	Marginal Unit Contribution	Total Contribution	Fixed Assets	Contribution Fixed Assets
	10	100	1.0	110	10	11.0	-7.0	1.0	3.0	-70	100	-0.70
	20	100	1.0	120	20	6.0	-2.0	1.0	3.0	-40	100	-0.40
Plant break-even →	30	100	1.0	130	30	4.3	-0.3	1.0	3.0	-10	100	-0.10
	40	100	1.0	140	40	3.5	0.5	1.0	3.0	20	100	0.20
Minimum variable cost/unit (five shifts/week) →	50	100	1.0	150	50	3.0	1.0	1.0	3.0	50	100	0.50
	60	100	1.1	166	60	2.8	1.2	1.6	2.4	74	100	0.74
	70	100	1.2	184	70	2.6	1.4	1.8	2.2	96	100	0.96
	80	100	1.3	204	80	2.55	1.45	2.0	2.0	116	100	1.16
	90	100	1.4	226	90	2.5	1.5	2.2	1.8	134	100	1.34
	100	100	1.5	250	100	2.5	1.5	2.4	1.6	150	100	1.50
	110	100	1.6	276	110	2.5	1.5	2.6	1.4	164	100	1.64
Minimum total cost/unit (12½ shifts/week) →	120	100	1.7	304	120	2.5	1.5	2.8	1.2	176	100	1.76
	130	100	1.8	334	130	2.6	1.4	3.0	1.0	186	100	1.86
	140	100	1.9	366	140	2.6	1.4	3.2	0.8	194	100	1.94
	150	100	2.0	400	150	2.7	1.3	3.4	0.6	200	100	2.00
	160	100	2.1	436	160	2.7	1.3	3.6	0.4	204	100	2.04
	170	100	2.2	474	170	2.8	1.2	3.8	0.2	206	100	2.06
Maximum contribution →	180	100	2.3	514	180	2.9	1.1	4.0	0.0	206	100	2.06
	190	100	2.4	556	190	2.9	1.1	4.2	-0.2	204	100	2.04
	200	100	2.5	600	200	3.0	1.0	4.4	-0.4	200	100	2.00
Absolute capacity (21 shifts/week) →	210	100	2.6	646	210	3.1	0.9	4.6	-0.6	194	100	1.94

Pro Forma Standard Costs per Unit

Manufacturing cost 2.5
Marketing and distribution 1.0

Contribution 0.5
Allocated costs 1.0
Profit B/T
Total sales price 5.0

where substantial marketing or research and development expenses are included in corporate expense.

The *cost* section of the production/facilities plan is basically a capital investment budget for the planning period. It should include some kind of factor for minor work-order capital costs that cannot be scheduled individually but that you know from past experience are going to occur. Some companies use a factor of 10 percent of net fixed assets annually to provide for such replacements, improvements, and capitalized repairs.

Profitability Plan

Your production people gave you a fixed investment forecast. You have a set of dollar sales objectives from which your finance people can predict fairly reliably what the working capital requirements will be. You therefore should know what the asset base is that will be required to achieve the declared sales and earnings objectives. Divide the earnings by the assets.

If your accounts will not provide sufficient information to track this performance in the past, at least calculate it for last year and estimate it for this year. This means you will have to allocate assets to SBUs. Your people are very likely to say this cannot be done. They are wrong. With a little common sense, it is not that difficult. Working capital should be straightforward. Shared fixed assets can be allocated on tonnage, machine hours, man-hours, square footage, or any other dimension that makes sense. Just do not spread everything as a percentage of sales dollars, because it will not tell you anything much. You may have to allocate corporate headquarters and a few other things that way, though.

For Additional Information

Multiplan, Victor Technologies.

Senior Analyst, Apple Computer.

Visicalc—Advanced, Visicorp.

Some of the software packages available for putting plans on microcomputers.

Eccles, R. G., "Control with Fairness in Transfer Pricing," *Harvard Business Review*, Vol. 61, No. 6 (November–December 1983), pp. 149–161.

There is no "objective" solution to the transfer pricing problem. It both reflects and influences strategy and management style. A good treatment.

Pennington, M., and Cohen, S., "Michael Porter Speaks on Strategy," *Planning Review* (January 1982), pp. 8–12, 36–39.

An interview in which Porter says there are only three basic competitive strategies: differentiation, cost leadership, focus.

8
Cascade or Deluge?

When we mean to build,
We first survey the plot, then draw the model;
And when we see the figure of the house,
Then must we rate the cost of the erection;
Which if we find outweighs ability,
What do we then but draw anew the model
In fewer offices, or at last desist to build at all?

—WILLIAM SHAKESPEARE

"We made too many action plans, and we got bogged down."
Maybe you did make too many action plans. By using a
structured approach to examining the nature of the business
and agreeing on directions for development, you may just
have uncovered so many things that ought to be done that
you tried to do everything at once and exceeded the available
resources. Then again, you may have gotten so tangled up in
actions that you forgot the structure of the objectives.

All planning specialists, myself included, have seen so
many elegant plans, intricate intellectual constructions,
gather dust on a shelf because they were never translated into
actionable terms that they tend to harp on the theme: "Your
planning is not done until you carry it through to the action
step!" Who is going to do what, when?

123

Action Planning

But action planning is such a simple, convenient, and effective device for getting things done that it tends to be seductive. Deciding what should be done is the hard part. Figuring out how to do it is often pretty much straight administrative skill. The action plan is done in large part to protect the person who writes it, the person who has accepted the responsibility for attaining certain results, a certain objective. It is also done in order to make possible a reasonably accurate estimate of the cost of attaining that objective. But it is the result, the objective, that is important. So maybe there were not too many action plans. Maybe they were done too soon before the objectives were nailed down. Maybe they were done by the wrong people or in the wrong degree of detail.

Go back to fundamentals for a minute. Planning works from ends to means, from objectives to actions. You structure the objectives; the actions follow from the objectives. You administer actions; you plan objectives.

Now some arithmetic! The chief executive officer has perhaps five or six key result objectives for which he or she alone can have personal responsibility: total sales, earnings, profitability, and two or three lines of development of the enterprise. The CEO may, if he or she chooses, draw up action plans for those objectives, laying out on a time line the actions that must be taken to fulfill his or her responsibilities. He or she will do this primarily to make life more orderly and to provide a control framework by which progress toward the objectives can be measured.

If the CEO has ten people on the planning team, each is likely to be personally responsible for eight or ten objectives. If they write action plans for each objective, we are now getting up around 100 action plans in total. If you hold a planning meeting and discuss each action plan for only ten minutes, it will require more than two full eight-hour days—with no time for coffee breaks, phone calls, lunch, or discussion of football scores. This is patently unrealistic. How did we get into this mess?

You have a planning team, a planning committee. Planning can be done sequentially if you have a strong CEO or a very good planning coordinator, but team planning has become almost universal. It seems to save time in the long run, it makes for better communications, and it facilitates commitment. Furthermore, it is participative, which is a very popular word these days. More important it brings the perceptions and judgments of a number of people to the planning process. Most businesses and their environments today are just too complex for one cranium to encompass all their aspects, and the hazards of tunnel vision are too daunting.

But how big is the planning team? Some companies try to work with a committee of 14 or 16. They want to get everyone involved, but they fail to do the arithmetic that reminds them that 16 people with a half hour of comment each shoots a day. Sixteen people with ten action plans apiece are completely unmanageable. Eventually, if planning survives, they are faced with the painful task of eliminating people from the planning committee. Many people should be involved in producing a corporate plan, but they cannot all sit around one conference table.

The more comprehensive—which is to say, the more sophisticated—your planning becomes, the more essential it is to you to develop procedures for propagating the planning process through the organization without having everyone discuss everything in one room. The converse of this rule is that you must assure the flow of information to your central conference room, but it must be progressively screened so that only the critical material comes through.

Hierarchy of Objectives

Which brings us, by a rather roundabout path, to the hierarchy of objectives. No matter what the style of management, objectives must relate to one another in a hierarchy—that is, they must be conceived in a structure that builds toward a few really important accomplishments. That is how you get a sense of direction and a concentrated thrust in the business. And the hierarchy must be fairly steep for the simple reason that the human mind can deal only with a certain number of variables. Computers help, but not that much. What we are talking about here is comparable to, but not identical with, the familiar "span of control" doctrine. You might properly call it the "span of comprehension."

Two of the basic skills that must be mastered for successful planning are *aggregation* and *disaggregation*. The subject came up first in the discussion of setting up SBUs. Top management cannot plan strategy for every single product catalog item. It must find some rational way to group items into a manageable number of aggregate units. This is necessary, not only to think about them constructively, but in order to set up control points at which their situation can be monitored. The same kind of problem and the same process exist at every level of management.

Aggregation

There are no fixed rules for the bases on which aggregation is done. About the best you can say is that you should combine things into units that seem most manageable. This is subjective to the extent that it presupposes that they will be managed in a certain way, but that is not a relevant objection. The point is: What is really important? What do you really want to monitor and control? Do you really want to open a West Coast sales office, or do you want to increase your market share on the Pacific Coast? Or is what you really care about increasing unit sales by 15 percent? It depends on where you sit. If you are the president, you want the total sales growth and the other matters are contributory results or subobjectives. If you are the sales manager, one of your developmental objectives may be to penetrate the Pacific Coast market. If you are the western regional manager, you have to get the office set up. Wherever you sit, thinking through these cause and effect chains will do some of the aggregation for you and you can concentrate on matters of direct concern to you.

What number of aggregates should you have? Individuals seem to differ somewhat in the number of variables they can handle simultaneously. Psychologists say the average is around 6 to 8. Let's be generous and say 10 to 12, but probably not much more than that. For a company to say it has 20 or 30 key result objectives is a contradiction in terms. There cannot be that many *key* dimensions to a business. The people just have not thought it through and are going to end up doing a little bit of everything.

Disaggregation

Now to turn the coin over! Once you have decided what the six or eight or ten results are that are really important to you, then you will want to disaggregate: segment those objectives into subobjectives that are easier to manage and control. The way you break down the job is in fact the strategy. You will do lots of this and a little bit of that, this sooner and that later. Someone else might go at it differently, which makes neither of you right nor wrong. That other person just sees the structure differently. However, one way may be easier than the other, or faster, or less expensive. That is why the skill with which an objective is segmented into subobjectives in many ways is the essence of management competence. If the subobjectives do not add up to the principal objective—in other words, if all the subobjectives are achieved but the principal objective is not—there has been a critical failure in judgment. On the other hand, if some subobjectives are really not essential to achieve the central objective, there has been a waste of resources. This is the "necessary and sufficient" rule. Do everything that needs to be done and nothing that is unnecessary.

Now to get back into operational terms. We have postulated that you have, perhaps, five key result objectives—the Big Three and possibly two developmental objectives. You have disaggregated the Big Three into strategic business units. One developmental objective you aggregated by saying you want to establish an export business and did not specify whether in Europe or Latin America or both. The development task force did the disaggregating in its program proposal. You want to shift your business away from dependence on the construction industry cycles but did not specify where it should go. That came in the program proposal. You might have set different developmental objectives, but you didn't, and so you have already defined some aspects of your general strategy.

The sales and earnings objectives within the SBUs further define your strategy. You will get most of your sales growth out of one SBU, but most of your earnings out of another, and will gradually withdraw from a third. Those are the really important decisions that the top managers as a group—the planning committee—made. They made them in consideration of the feasibility of the programs proposed in the SBU plan. Those programs represent the next level of disaggregation. You cannot go beyond this level of disaggregation because you won't have time.

Assume that you have six SBUs. You have six marketing plans and six production/facilities plans. Ultimately you will have six financial plans. You also have two development plans. That makes 20 plans. Each of those can be expressed as an action plan, which merely means spreading them out along a time line with due dates, review dates, approvals, responsibilities, and, of course, cost data. The action steps on these plans should be only those that the planning committee itself is interested in. Further detail will appear in other documentation.

If the planning committee gives careful consideration to the plans at this level of aggregation and designs its control procedures accordingly, it will have plenty to do and the chances are good that it will do the job well. If the members try to get down into greater degrees of detail, they will be diverted, possibly confused, probably overloaded.

Participation and Iteration

Notice particularly that these action plans are not designed around the planning meeting table. Some other group, either in the hierarchy or ad hoc, is asked to prepare them for review and approval by the planning committee. This is where your participative management and the iteration that planners talk about come in. The person whose name is put alongside the objective has the responsibility to involve anyone he or she thinks could contribute to the achievement of that objective. The person responsible disaggregates the objective into the segments he or she thinks are most manageable. If that person is a sales manager, he or she may set up subobjectives for individual sales regions, new products, or new territories, or may segment by classes of customers or by further breakdown of product groups within the SBU—whatever breakdown he or she feels can be dealt with most effectively. This is where skill and judgment as a manager will be applied. When the person responsible brings those subobjectives in with the marketing plan, their pattern and balance will define the approach, the strategy for achieving this objective, as much as all the text that goes along with them. This is the plan.

The document the person brings back to the planning committee—what I have called a plan—should more properly be called a plan proposal. It should represent the best opinion and judgment in the organization—or outside of it, for that matter. This is the kind of submittal a committee can deal with. Committee members can appraise the evaluation of the situation, consider the reasonableness of the objectives, and critique the appropriateness of the strategy. They could not create the plan in a planning meeting, but they can assess it in one. If the committee accepts the proposal, then it is worthwhile for everyone to spend the additional effort to detail out the ultimate action plans, sharpen up the cost estimates, and propagate the hierarchy of objectives and action plans to additional levels of the organization. If he or she has not already done so, the regional sales manager may set another set of objectives for each sales office and the office sales manager may set objectives for individual salespeopie, although not necessarily for the full planning period.

Now your hierarchy of objectives has cascaded down through the entire organization. Anywhere and everywhere along the line, people may have written action plans for their own convenience and protection or for the reassurance of their immediate superiors. However, the only ones that the planning committee sees are the ones to attain the objectives at the level of aggregation directly below the key result objectives. The other action plans are reviewed and ap-

proved, at the appropriate levels in the chain of command—
that is, by the immediate superior of the person responsible
for the action plan.

Negotiated Management

Of course, you can create the appearance of a hierarchy of
objectives by simply dealing objectives out like a deck of
cards. You can even put them all in a book, but that book may
turn out to be a fantasy. Negotiated objectives are much more
likely to be realistic, and the subordinate has a psychological
investment in achieving them. You can reinforce that investment with an incentive system if you want. Undoubtedly,
some people are better negotiators than others—both up and
down. You will always have some managers whose notion of
negotiating is "take it or leave it." And some sharpies who
will chisel down the price. But on the whole you will be on
more solid ground. This is the technique of managing by
objectives, but unlike most MBO systems, this one is tied into
a logical structure of objectives that builds to an apex of the
main strategic thrusts of the enterprise.

Negotiated responsibilities are more compatible with the
spirit of the times. The upcoming generations are very reluctant to take authoritarian direction. Some people say we are
coming into what they call "the contract society," in which all
organizational relationships will be on a contractual basis: so
much performance for so much compensation. Employees
will be almost indistinguishable from subcontractors. If that
is where we are going, you might as well get ready.

At least as important is the feedback you get from this
negotiating process, if you are careful to keep the channels
open. Most minor shortfalls, or gaps, that arise should be
accommodated well down in the organization. If that San
Francisco sales office manager cannot get commitments from
his salespeople to add up to his sales objective for one SBU,
he may scurry around and make a few crucial sales calls
himself. He might even put on another salesperson if he can
justify it. But if somebody has made a real bad estimate and
the sales potential is just not there the sales manager is not

going to take the rap for an unattainable performance. He is
going to go back to the regional manager and renegotiate this
objective. And if the regional manager cannot pick up the
slack with sales in Arizona, she is going to buck the problem
on up the line. This is where the strict accountability comes
in. If people view these objectives as targets, which if you
don't hit you get your wrists slapped, they are inclined to shut
up and take their chances and hope for a lucky break. But if
these are established as contractual commitments, the responsible people are going to react up front. You will not
necessarily get any more performance one way or the other.
The difference is that with the contractual style you find out
about any problems in advance rather than get disappointing
surprises after the fact. If you find out in advance, there is a
chance to do something about it. After the target has been
missed, there is nothing left but recriminations and finger-
pointing excuses.

Be sure you leave time in your planning calendar for this
loop to close—for these negotiations to proceed and the feedback to come in. It may shake up your preconceptions, but it
will not change the reality, only what you do about it. If you
cannot get commitments that will add up to your key objectives, change the objectives. No use kidding yourself.

Probabilities

What do you do about the "possibles" and "probables" that
you are working on? Do you count them in as gap fillers?
Some people say that you should overdesign your gap fillers
by 50 or 100 percent to allow for the inevitable failures. Some
write the expected results down by a probability factor and
then add up the adjusted values. Neither of these techniques
is statistically sound or psychologically wise. With a small
number of items, probability statistics do not work. To tell
people that if their project does not work somebody else will
bail them out is poor psychology.

Don't count anything until at least one person is convinced it can be done and is willing to put his or her name on
it. Then count all of it. This is the "champion" system that has

been getting a lot of attention lately, and it is a valid principle. Someone who is on the line for a result can do amazing things, particularly if you have shown confidence enough in this person to factor his or her results into the plans. You will still have failures, and when you do, you will have to write them out of your plans. Presumably, by that time you will have some new project to put in its place. But don't marry the second spouse until you divorce the first. It will do wonders to concentrate your attention. If you want to be prudent, be modest in your expectations from development projects. Then let probabilities work for you by assuring that some projects will exceed your expectations by a substantial margin.

The project that does not yet have a champion or that you are not yet ready or able to pursue all out should stay in your research, product development, or market analysis budget as an expense item. Keep the pipeline filled. Let projects queue up, if you should be so lucky as to have an excess. But take them sequentially in order of attractiveness. Do not try to fiddle around with everything at the same time.

Costs

If you have good cost estimates in the action plans at the lowest level of subobjectives, you can accumulate costs up through the hierarchy and see your costs at any level of objective. This can be very informative. Most objectives can be achieved at some cost. The question is: Is the result worth the cost? If your objective cascade is well structured, you can make that comparison at multiple levels. It could save you some resources and improve your overall performance. That is what you are after, isn't it?

For Additional Information

Kastens, M. L., *Redefining the Manager's Job*. New York: AMACOM, 1980, Appendix B.

All about the "contract society."

Macrae, N., "The Company Entrepreneurial Revolution," *The Economist* (December 25, 1976).

Macrae has been following the trend toward contractual management for some time. He reports on it periodically.

Likert, R., *The Human Organization.* New York: McGraw-Hill Book Company, 1967.

Likert's research showed that even in the early 1960s authoritarian management did not work very well. This is even more true in the 1980s.

Polacek, R. J., "Strategic Errors of Smaller Companies," *ChemTech*, Vol. 13, No. 6 (June 1983), pp. 340–344.

On the relationship of objectives and strategies. Not much new but extremely well stated. Good "refresher" material.

9

Keep Up the Pressure

For every human problem there is a solution that is neat, simple, and wrong.

—H. L. MENCKEN

How is that sense of urgency, which we talked about in connection with action plans to correct weaknesses? Have the individuals to whom you assigned the projects come up with acceptable action proposals, and have these been approved? Are they being implemented?

It should not be necessary to have a meeting of the whole planning team to approve an action plan. The CEO may be willing to take that responsibility personally. Or maybe it can be handled at a regular meeting of the executive committee or by a subcommittee designated for the purpose. The important thing is to have an explicit approval procedure after the proposal is submitted. There should be a specific time and place at which the "go" button is pushed, the necessary expenditures of time and money authorized, and the milestones for progress review established.

As has been said, this is an activity entirely independent of and parallel to the total planning process. However, weaknesses were defined as problems that impair the ability to attain one or more of the key result objectives. They should be cross-referenced to the pertinent objective and appear there as a subobjective in the overall plan. If, for example, the problem is excessive raw material inventories, the correction by definition is essential to achieve the profitability objective. The promised results for the action plan therefore should appear under the profitability KRO. If you cannot find a place to put a weakness action plan under a KRO, it suggests that maybe the problem is not so critical as you thought it was.

Any threats that were uncovered in your environmental analysis and that were deemed to warrant action plans should be treated exactly like action plans to correct weaknesses, because the risk was considered to be both immediate and serious.

The simplest way to code these action plans for cross-referencing is to number your weaknesses and threats and then designate the corresponding action plans as W-1, W-2, and so on for weaknesses, and T-1, T-2, and so on for threats. But keep them in a separate section of the planning book, because they have overriding priority and the responsibility for overseeing their implementation goes directly up to the chief executive officer.

You may encounter the objection that some of the weaknesses involve operational matters, and it is quite possible that they do. The point is irrelevant. You have identified the problem as threatening the vitality of the entire enterprise. As such, it becomes the concern of the very top management. The matter has been taken out of the normal administrative procedure and given transcendent priority.

When you have the action proposals before you, you may find that one or more of the weaknesses can apparently be corrected in the current year even before the present plan is completed. This is embarrassing. If the problem is so serious and it can be solved so quickly, the question naturally arises: Why was it allowed to develop? This is a good question. Obviously, this is not the subject of a long-term strategic plan. Well, be thankful that it is being handled now, and count the benefit as a by-product of the planning process. But you are entitled to ask the question.

Investigation

As the result of your environmental analysis, you may have asked someone to investigate some external situation because no one really knew enough about it to make reasonable assumptions. The first thing you want the assignee to tell you is whether it is important enough for you to take some action. You have to rely on that person's diligence and judgment to make that assessment. What you really need is a "white paper" on the situation. Depending on what the investigator finds, you will need it either right away or when the person gets around to it. You would prefer to have it right away, though. If there are recommendations for action, then you have to get together with your planning committee and decide what you want to do. If there are no such recommendations, the analysis can merely be circulated to the interested parties, and at your next regular meeting, you can decide whether to stay on top of it or forget it.

You are not going to add any contingency plans into your numbers anyway, so you do not need them until you wrap up the entire plan; then add them as an appendix.

The one thing you want to be sure of is that every assignment you make is completed in an appropriate time. Do not let any of them slide, or your organizational discipline will be lost and you will have great difficulty in implementing any aspect of your plans.

Strengths

What about the programs you assigned to exploit strengths? If there were any real hot ones, they are probably reflected in added development objectives. Most of the rest will probably be incorporated in SBU objectives. Since you have already said that these are probably high-priority prospects, to the extent that someone is already working on them, you have a head start. If it has turned out on further investigation that you overvalued the strength, you can drop the idea, and you still will have eliminated it a little sooner than you otherwise would have. If you have some that do not fit in any SBU and do not seem important enough to set up as key development objectives, keep them around for "stocking stuffers." If when you get to the final stages of your planning, you have any talent left over—particularly a young person you would like to test—turn him or her loose on one of them and see what comes out. But get the proposal finished in writing, with numbers so you know just what it is you are deferring or reactivating. If you have a champion who gets really steamed up over a project, it will probably end up as a development objective. Enthusiasm is a very powerful resource.

Opportunities

Did you spot any hot opportunities when you did your environmental analysis? When the task force comes in with its action plan proposal to exploit the possibilities, you should be able to decide almost at a glance what you should do with it. Once in a while, one will come in that is so overwhelmingly attractive that you will immediately convert it into a corporate development KRO. Much more commonly, though, you will want to simply table the proposal until you get all the pieces of the plan together and see if you have any resources leftover. You may, however, authorize continued exploratory work pending a go/no-go decision, but for the present, you will not count anything but preliminary costs in your figures.

The basic message of this little intermezzo in the long-range planning process is to keep procedures on a short rein, follow up, and establish a culture in which people expect to fulfill their commitments because they know you expect them to. There is no substitute for it.

10
Costs and Consequences

These are the times that try men's souls.

—THOMAS PAINE

Your people should be pretty good at writing action plans by now. It is useful to write action plans at any level in your hierarchy of objectives, but the critical ones are those at the lowest level, where the work actually gets done. That is also where the numbers can be the most precise.

A lot of people use action plans regularly for scheduling and control purposes, but they stop there. They get only half the value. One of the reasons for doing action plans is to cost out tactics to see just what you are spending to attain any level of objective. Then you can do a cost/benefit analysis. For that, you need two things. You must know the cost and the benefit—the objective must be specific and measurable. If your action plans do not give you those two ingredients, they are not doing their job.

Also, in order to do a meaningful cost/benefit assessment, you need total cost, not just out-of-pocket. In most action plans, the biggest cost item is the time of people who are already on the payroll. If you use this resource for one purpose, it is not available for some other. It is the resource that

138

you are most likely to overspend. You may want to calculate incremental cost for budgetary purposes, but make a total human resources budget, too.

This will take some practice. Everybody underestimates how long things will take. Making yourself write it down month by month helps you be more realistic. Be sure you count everybody. If you are going to introduce a new product to the sales force, you have to charge yourself for all the time of the salespeople at the sales meeting, not just for that of the new product manager. If a cost-reduction program at the plant requires training production people, the project uses up, not just the time of the trainer, but the time of the trainees, too. If you set up a research screening or steering committee, that will tie up the time of a lot of expensive people. You'll be surprised how expensive committees are. Use a simple form, such as the one in Figure 9, for allocating human resources.

Cost/Benefit Analyses

Is it worthwhile to do a cost/benefit analysis on every action plan? Yes, if you keep it simple and do not get carried away. Theoretically, you could do a discounted cash flow (DCF) analysis on each action project. That would be a lot of work. You will do a DCF on the big capital commitment projects anyway. For the others, a break-even or pay-back period calculation is quite adequate. Remember, it is pointless to strive for great precision in these kinds of calculations because your estimates are not that exact. Two, or at most three, significant figures are plenty. You want to know whether pay-back is in one year, two years, or five years, not whether it is the second Tuesday in June of the second year. For budget purposes, you will want to differentiate capitalized items and expense items, but you can do a cost/benefit on a strictly cash flow basis and mix the two kinds of outlays together. By sticking to a cash flow break-even, you avoid most of the arguments over how long you can count the benefits from a given action.

What you are really trying to find out is whether the game

Figure 9.   Resource allocation schedule.

Month	Human Resources (Man-Days)			Money	
	Managerial	Professional	Clerical	Expense	Capital
Total					

is worth the candle. Most action plans that do not break-even within a three- or five-year planning period are not worth doing anyway. The exceptions would be ones that have major long-range development implications. Those you may have to carry as cost items to the end of the planning period, but you probably also will have an extensive project analysis of the venture anyhow. Do your cost/benefit analysis for the mental discipline of forcing your people to face up to the total cost of the proposed project and to quantify the possible returns if the project is successful. This is not a matter of detailed cost accounting, but of management perspective.

Even if you avoid controversy over the longevity of benefits, you will still have some problems over what numbers to use. You will want to use "total" costs, but just what are total costs? In general, you do not need to charge a project with transferred fixed assets since those can be considered as "sunk" costs and not chargeable to the project. However, if the facility could be used for some other purpose or even sold, you really should assess the opportunity cost equal to the cash flow that an alternative use could have generated. A parallel situation arises if you plan to divert a production facility to some experimental runs. If this is to be done during a normal operating day, then the value of the lost production should be charged. If, on the other hand, the experiments can be run at a time when the equipment would ordinarily be idle, then you incur only out-of-pocket costs.

What about overheads? You will definitely want to charge the cost of fringe benefits along with your labor costs, but your usual formula for allocating other overhead is likely to be inappropriate for many special projects. A little common sense is in order here. You might add a somewhat arbitrary 10 percent or so to total cost for overhead, or if your burden rates are not very high, you might just skip the whole thing.

In calculating your personnel costs, for goodness sake, do not try to use individual salary figures. Use average daily or weekly rates, including fringes, for three or four classes of employees and multiply them out from your human resources budget. Remember, you are trying to get a general perspective on the situation, not make a dollar-by-dollar accounting.

Deciding how to credit benefits can be tricky. The principle is staightforward: Determine the net cash flow that will occur with the proposed project, and compare it with the cash flow without it. If you keep that principle firmly in mind, it helps. However, as a practical matter, it is not always so easy to determine those two cash streams. The trouble is that a lot of different things are happening at the same time, and the results are comingled. You want to avoid double counting. A little "logic chopping" will usually see you through.

Let's say you have an action plan to open a new regional sales office, and during the same period, you plan to introduce a new product line. You can estimate the sales you expect to get out of that region without the new products and credit them to the first project and then credit the total sales you expect from the new products to the second. That is not strictly rigorous because the new product sales would have been less if the additional sales office had not existed, but it will not lead you too far astray.

What about defensive projects—improved quality or upgraded field service, for instance? If they are truly necessary defensive moves, there is an underlying assumption that if you do not do them you will eventually lose sales. You can quantify the value of that lost business. Maybe you cannot afford to provide better quality or more service. Maybe it would be cheaper and just as effective to cut prices.

Some action plans aim at results that are truly not calculable. Here is where you want to be very careful, because this is fertile ground for pious hopes and "Boy, wouldn't it be nice if . . ." The first thing you want to do is be sure that the benefits are, in fact, noncalculable.

- You want to improve morale on the shop floor. Why? Sure, you would like everyone to be happy, but where is current low morale hurting you? Low productivity? High reject rate? Excessive turnover? Those things can be quantified and costed.
- You would like greater depth in management. So would almost everybody. But what really is your risk exposure? How badly could you be hurt and, specifically, where? Can you really justify that junior management development program?
- You want greater recognition in the market. Will that really sell more products or just give the executives more presence at the country club?

There is a lot of work to be done. Can you really justify committing resources to efforts for which you cannot identify what you are trying to accomplish? Admittedly, everything cannot be measured in dollars and cents, but there really should be some effort to determine whether the results sought are commensurate with the effort involved. This is a step in the planning routine where truly the process is more important than the product.

Action Plans and Budgets

You may as well do a fairly decent job of cost/benefit analysis on action plans because, when it comes around to budget time, you will have to do it anyway if the budget is to be anything more than a ceremonial ritual. You do not have to write action plans to do the things you have been doing all along. The action plans represent new activities. Thus, their costs and their consequences are additive to the historical budget trends. Consequently, if you make up a trial budget by conventional extrapolative techniques, you should then be able to list your action plans line by line underneath and make the appropriate additions and subtractions until you come to a net budget at the bottom. Psychologically, it is most effective if you list the cost-saving actions first, followed by the income-producing ones. Nowadays, this can all be done on a personal computer with standard programs, which makes it very easy to revise and refine values as the number crunching proceeds. It makes the budgeting process both easier and more meaningful.

This kind of budgeting can be done at any level of aggregation appropriate to the individual level of responsibility. With the availability of stock computer programs, it is entirely possible for anyone with budget responsibility to have his or her own breakdown for the activities he or she is responsible for. Without too much manipulation, it is possible to compile these individual budgets into an overall corporate budget.

This facility for aggregation is the final function of action planning. We have given considerable emphasis to the value of action plans for scheduling and control purposes, and it is true that that value can be realized if the plans never leave the originator's desk. But if you finish the job, you will be able to determine money and human resources commitments to any segment of the business and you can see how they relate to the total resources of the corporation. This is a very powerful insight that is virtually impossible to get any other way.

11
Does It Add Up?

The great tragedy of Science—the slaying of a beautiful hypothesis by an ugly fact.

—THOMAS HUXLEY

When you get together for your third major set of planning sessions, you should all really know what you are talking about and be ready to make firm commitments. The time required for these sessions will be almost directly proportional to the number of SBUs you have. Each SBU should first be considered separately as if it were a freestanding business. The individual plans should be distributed a week or two before the meeting so there will be no need to review them word by word. Even so, a little background and general exposition plus questions and discussion will take a couple of hours, maybe half a day for each SBU. If some of the plans are shot down or are not credible, or if the results are not acceptable, you have a procedural problem. It is usually not practical to adjourn the whole meeting to a later date while the offending plan is reworked. You will have to plug in the unsatisfactory numbers pro forma, with the understanding that a subsequent special meeting will be needed to consider revisions and recalculation of the totals. You may encounter some other matters that will have to be recycled later in the

144

process anyway. Unfortunately, the world is not always as neat as we would like it to be.

When the SBU presentations have been completed, add their sales, earnings, and profitability objectives together. (If the plans are well prepared, this can be done in advance.) This arithmetic will give you your first general impression of how realistic your KROs are.

SBU Sales Objectives

How close do the combined SBU sales objectives come to the corporate sales objective? Remember that the SBU plans already have some development KROs within the scope of the SBU. What are the chances that the corporate development KROs will generate substantial sales soon enough to fill the gap? You will know better when you get the development project proposals later on, but does the order of magnitude look feasible? If not, you could tell your SBU people to go back and do some more Quadrant 4 thinking (see Figure 5), but that is a pretty iffy proposition. If they did not come up with the ideas spontaneously, anything you squeeze out of them by directive is likely to be questionable. You had better start thinking about some additional corporate development KROs or be prepared to scale back your corporate objectives. You could start by going back over some of those opportunity and strength ideas you laid aside earlier.

Earnings Objectives

To combine the contribution objectives for the SBUs, you will have to make the appropriate adjustments for corporate charges and taxes in order to compare them with the earnings objectives you set for your corporation. You will note that to do this somebody has to set objectives for administrative charges, corporate research and development, and any other deductions that will be made from the SBUs combined contribution. This is where you look at your administrative plan.

Now what have you got? If the sum of the parts is substantially greater than the intended whole, you may have some discretionary funds that you can "invest" in long-term developments with payoffs beyond the planning period—maybe accelerate some of those corporate developments. What about the SBU that came in well in excess of the corporate earnings expectations? Should you invest some of that unexpected margin in moving more aggressively into that market? What if you cut prices, perhaps selectively? What if you spent some more on marketing? Would it help to give salespeople special incentives to push the products? Can you afford to expand your market geographically? All good thoughts.

If you do not have that slack in earnings, you may be in trouble, because you still have some development projects that you have not counted in that will be a drain on those earnings, certainly in the early years. If the SBUs together cannot promise you the earnings growth you think you need, then you may have an earnings gap. If you also had a sales gap, you might say that the gap-filling sales will provide the additional earnings to make up the earnings gap. It could happen at least three or five years out if you can get some new businesses up and running in that time, but it may be tough. Usually, new activities are very slow in generating substantial earnings. It will be easier to get sales than earnings. The most probable way to fill both gaps simultaneously would be through an acquisition. But that would almost certainly make the profitability objective harder to achieve, as you will see.

What about SBUs that are not coming anywhere close to corporate earnings objectives? They may have to be restructured. Is there any way costs can be cut? Presumably, the production people have good reasons for their cost calculations. Let them defend their numbers. Not infrequently someone from another department can spot a flaw in the reasoning, sometimes the result of a misunderstanding of the product requirements. If you cannot shake the cost figures, then what can be changed to improve the situation? What would happen to sales if you raised prices? Is all of the marketing expense justified if margins are that low? Is the product overdesigned? How much market would you sacrifice if you cut back on the specifications?

Look into these possibilities, but before you make any final decisions, check to see what assets are behind this SBU. It may be a low-margin but still very profitable business if there is very little in the way of assets that could be pulled out and employed better somewhere else. Do not, however, be diverted by the argument that "the SBU contributes to overhead." That is not a valid consideration for the long haul. This SBU does not have the earnings potential you thought it had, and for that reason alone, it must be rethought.

Profitability Objectives

Now we come to the moment of truth—the profitability objectives, the return on assets. This is the measure by which you can compare the performance of all the SBUs regardless of the peculiarities of their respective businesses. If you have one or two SBUs that are only slightly below par but have been more or less steady for years, the best you can probably expect is to hold them steady. But what about the problem children whose profitability is half or one-third of what you have set as the corporate average. Don't turn your back on them. You have some real tough decisions to make. If they are adolescent-type products that are just beginning to hit their stride, fine. How soon do you expect them to yield a respectable return? But what about the persistent underperformers? Can you see any chance to double or triple their profitability? If you have some ideas you want to try, put a time limit on them. Give them two years to get well. If they do not make it by then, have a contingency plan to get out. If you really do not have credible ideas, plan an orderly withdrawal. Milk the business if possible. If not, liquidate it. If you can reemploy the resources, particularly the people, to more profitable activities, it will help a lot in achieving your overall profitability objective. But this may mean that you will have to go back and change some of your sales and earnings numbers.

If you can, plan an orderly withdrawal. Return to that

SBU's marketing plan and cut it back. Raise prices to discourage customers. At least you can get the working capital back and sweeten your margins somewhat. Does cutting back the sales volume save you any new fixed investment in your facilities plan? You certainly cannot afford to invest new money in this business. Take it out. Any present fixed investment in this SBU will be depreciating and in five years will be less of a drag on your overall performance. If you can cash out some of the fixed assets under acceptable terms, fine.

As a test net out from your total business the assets and the earnings associated with the poorest performing SBU, and recalculate your overall profitability. It might look like a pretty good business that way. That is where you want to get, although it may take a while. Maybe you should consider some more pruning.

If you do not have any identifiable "dogs" in your SBUs and you still cannot see acceptable profitability, examine the basic logic of your KROs. Is it reasonable to expect earnings to grow faster than sales when you are planning all this market expansion and development activity? If for some reason you must have the growth in earnings, maybe you must cut back on some of your more ambitious expansion plans. If that's the conclusion, then you need a major recycle—but maybe you are just not doing things right. If you are convinced that no more can be squeezed out of production costs and believe that the marketing budgets are justified, there is only one other place to look: the administrative plan. Does it use historical ratios? Is there any reason why those ratios have to hold? Maybe you can squeeze a few percentage points out there to get you back on the track. Is it conceivable to save enough in administrative expense to make that much difference overall? If your accounting is such that your burden rate is only 5 or 6 percent, the chance of bringing it down by as much as a full percent is probably pretty slim. If the rate is 15 or 20 percent, though, it should be entirely possible. If you think that the solution does lie in administrative expenses, get someone on it right away and see what skeletons you can turn up. You might be well advised to get an outsider to do it, though, because this is where the bureaucracy is likely to be most thoroughly entrenched and the most draconian measures will be required to make any changes. Probably that is why this is usually the last place people look for savings.

If when you take a look at those expense allocations you find that they have been calculated by taking the present budget numbers and simply applying an inflation factor, you are in worse trouble than you thought. The most prevalent misconception in management is that overhead costs can be held approximately constant as a business grows. This never happens. Everybody reads Parkinson, but nobody believes him. It takes considerable skill and effort to keep overhead from growing *faster* than the company.

Asset Management

If you cannot get the net earnings figure up, remember there is another factor in your profitability equation: the investment base. Unless a company has recently had a major campaign on it, there is almost no organization that cannot squeeze something out of its working capital. Of course, some companies have higher working capital requirements than others, so there is more to squeeze. I know it is in all the textbooks, but frankly, cash management, credit management, and inventory control are not often well done. It took a long time for Americans to realize that one of the "secrets" of Japanese profitability is their "just-in-time" inventory system. Take a good hard look at your current asset accounts. A couple of day's shortening of average receivables or an extra inventory turn or two can sometimes do wonders for profitability.

And take a look around at your fixed assets, too. Do you have any nonproducing assets that could be cashed in? Or even some marginally productive ones that could be sold off and their intermediate product bought from an outside supplier? Reversing integration is not always a bad idea—even though there does not seem to be any name for it except "disintegration," which somehow does not sound right.

Realize, too, that there is almost certainly a favorable bias in the profitability of the later years. Your projected capital expenditures will almost inevitably tail off in the later years of the plan because you have no idea what kind of capacity you will be buying at that time to produce stuff out beyond the last year of the plan. When it comes to calculating profitabilities, this will introduce a double distortion. First, your asset figure will be unrealistically low, and second, your depreciation charges will be understated because some of that new investment will begin to be depreciated during the planning period. This is one of the causes of the euphoria induced by some long-range plans, the feeling that prosperity is just around the corner. People are chasing an ever receding horizon.

There is no truly rigorous way you can accommodate this difficulty. Certainly, you can anticipate if and when your sales objectives will run you out of capacity and provide for new plant investment at costs inflated by an appropriate factor. You can provide for work-order-level minor capital cost using an experience factor. But you know that it is highly likely that there will be some new fixed investments out in those later years that you just cannot foresee. Calculating your profitability on the undepreciated value of the assets cushions the effect somewhat; but in a smaller company, when you do retire a facility, it produces a step-up in profitability that is completely unrealistic. The practice works better in a big company, such as DuPont. The large number of items damps the jumps. After you get out about three years in the analysis, you can finesse the whole thing by using a minimum new fixed investment figure that is a percentage of sales or earnings based on past experience without regard to specific budget items. Such recourse is a kind of admission of defeat, but it does provide some protection against false hopes. If you do not do some such thing, be forewarned that the profitability in the later years of the plan is probably unrealistically high.

If even with this optimistic bias you cannot see where the returns are going to come from, you had better bite the bullet and admit that the profits are just not available in your company's current situation. Your hypothesis did not stand the test. Reset your objectives at some reasonable and realizable level. Then spend the next year trying to figure out how to convert your company into an entirely different kind of business, and the next ten years doing it. It can be done, but it is not easy!

But, if when you add up all the SBU numbers, the total comes close to your corporate objectives—say, plus or minus 10 percent in five years—it indicates that there is plenty of opportunity in your present lines of business to get you where you want to go. There is no reason to go off chasing rabbits. You may need plenty of innovation within the SBUs in order to realize their full potential, but you want to be sure to take full advantage of that potential and not permit yourself to be distracted by adventures into new areas. You have very little planning gap at the corporate level.

If the sum of the SBU objectives is substantially more than the performance you had said would be creditable for the corporation, you have a special problem. Could you stand the pace that would result from fully exploiting all of each SBU's opportunities, or would it shake the place apart? This is a really serious question and deserves the most profound consideration. Almost every day *The Wall Street Journal* chronicles the fate of a company that was killed by success. You may have to go back and reconsider some of your policies, particularly those relating to financial structure and staffing. If you are not willing to change the nature of your enterprise, you had better stop right now and whittle back those SBUs. Remember: You are *designing* your future, not letting it run away with you. If you decide to throttle down, you do not just slow down everything. You narrow the focus of some of the SBUs—constrict the areas in which they compete, but let them go full bore in the areas in which they do compete. How do you decide which SBUs to whittle down? Why, the least profitable ones, of course!

Keep the following principle in mind as you review SBU plans: If push comes to shove, you really have no choice but to accept the SBU plan numbers as submitted. It is too late in this cycle to completely redo them anyway. Probably, you cannot change the numbers without changing the faces, and that you cannot do instantaneously either. If you change the numbers, they are now your numbers, not theirs. If you think the numbers are overoptimistic, you still have to accept them. Just be sure your control system enables you to track the results closely and that the responsible people know they will be held strictly accountable for performance. Then, if they cannot make their numbers, you may take some action, but you cannot second-guess them going in. They may even be right.

Development Objective Plans

Your development KROs may be the key to the viability of your enterprise. They almost certainly are the key to its vitality.

Your development task forces should have their proposals ready to present, although not necessarily with a detailed strategy. They should be able to state what the results should be and when they might be expected. The cost figures should be reasonably solid. In fact, they can be considered as control limits. By their nature, these numbers are not quite as "hard" as the others you have been dealing with and ideally should not have a make-or-break significance in the success of the overall plan for the next few years. If the situation is so badly out of shape that the development programs *must* work to keep the company healthy over the planning period, then they must have "crash" priority, the best people, the president's time, and all the resources they can use productively. It might be claimed that, if these outside-SBU objectives are that critical to the survival of the company, they should not be called "development" objectives but "salvage" objectives. That is a semantic quibble, though, and situations do arise that require some heroic actions outside of the conventional activities of the enterprise. However, such a situation usually also implies a need for the quickest possible results, and the quick fix is not necessarily the basis for a long-term strategy.

Remember, when you set up the development objectives, you were looking beyond the nominal planning horizon and were planning actions to modify the strategic posture of the company in order to expand its opportunities in the long term. In fact, you also realized that pursuing these objectives would be likely to have an unfavorable impact on short-term earnings and profitability.

So give these proposed development objective programs the most careful consideration. They contain the future of your corporation. As they used to tell the wagoneers starting out on the Oregon Trail, "Pick a good rut, because you are going to be in it a long time."

The young, successful, one-product company has the most difficult task when it sets a development objective for its second product. That development objective is, in effect, half of its entire plan. You know how often companies get in trouble making that second step. The more mature company faces a similar choice in less critical dimensions. Setting development objectives and planning their implementation is how a management actually grabs the wheel and steers the enterprise to where it wants to go. Don't let all those numbers in the SBU plans absorb your attention to the neglect of the really innovative aspects of your direction.

Details, Details, Details

Once you are convinced that your SBU and development plans are as sound as your skill, judgment, and circumstances can make them and that all the major pieces are mutually compatible and self-consistent, you can give everybody the go-ahead to work out the details. There is still a lot of fine tuning to do and chinks and gaps to be filled in. Have everyone disaggregate the objectives into further levels of subobjectives for as many layers of a hierarchy as is appropriate, and diffuse them down through the organization. Get the action plans written, agreed to, and *approved at appropriate levels of management,* not by the planning committee. Then feed the results and the confirmed numbers back up through the chain of responsibility, to be assembled and recorded by the planning coordinator and converted into financial forecasts by the financial officers.

You do not need to have another planning team meeting to go over all of this detail. In fact, your team members could not do this even if they wanted to. But be warned, this will work only if you can count on your people to do good staff work, to write good action plans, and to propagate their planning responsibilities to their subordinates in an effective way. You cannot start out planning this way. You must grow up to it.

Be sure to set a due date when the detail data must be in the coordinator's office. Some of it may still be pro forma—that is, estimated, particularly for the development objectives. But your planning person must have something to plug into the matrix. Given the structure, though, this person can always enter better data when they become available and make appropriate adjustments to the overall results. If the information is on a data processor, the planner can issue revisions every week if need be. Don't let that bother you if the revisions are not overwhelming. A plan should be a living document. Better that than a fancy volume gathering dust in the bottom drawer.

You can have a one-day wrap-up meeting of the planning team sometime in the fall, probably at the kickoff of the budget season. There should not be too much to do then except to lock everything into place so that the first year of the plan can be converted into a budget.

For Additional Information

Granger, C. H., "The Hierarchy of Objectives," *Harvard Business Review*, Vol. 42, No. 3 (May–June 1964), pp. 63–74.

Still the basic work on the subject. Not much has been added since.

Kastens, M. L., "Chicken and Egg: Management and Planning," *Planning Review* (May 1980), pp. 9–13.

The rationality of creating a hierarchy of objectives.

12
Practice, Practice, Practice

Give persons a function and responsibility then hold them accountable, and you'll be surprised with the results you get.

—IRVING SHAPIRO

Why do plans fail to get implemented? There are five primary reasons:

Inappropriate management style.
Inadequate delegation.
Awkward organization.
Lack of credibility.
Incompetence.

Lack of planning skills is not on the list because the intellectual and technical skills used in planning are not that difficult. It is the way those skills are used and tied into the management practice that determines the effectiveness of the planning process. Incompetence is at the bottom of the list—intentionally so. It is least likely to be the cause of problems.

Management Style

If planning is to take root and flourish in any organization, it must have a reasonably compatible environment. A bunch of inveterate hip-shooters is never going to get any good out of planning. They will feel uncomfortable with it. They won't believe in it. And obviously they will not follow a plan if they make one. If such a management ever tried planning, they probably would not keep it up for five years—and they are not reading this book anyhow.

However, there are other, less acute failures to properly imbed the planning function into the organizational culture. The most common is the semidetached planning process. The top managers go to some remote location for a week, maybe even less. They very thoughtfully consider and agree on the proper policies, objectives, and strategies for the enterprise. Then everybody goes back to work, and someone writes up the decisions and distributes them as a book. A year later, the group gets together again, dusts off the book, and checks to see if things worked out the way they wanted them to. Actually, this can do some good. It can do a lot of good in focusing attention, but it does not provide much assurance that the plans will be worked out. It is a little like going out to a rifle range, putting up a target, and, when the marksman has gotten himself settled in a firing position, taking down the target and telling him to fire at will. When he has emptied his clip, you put the target back up and count up the score.

To get the full value out of planning, it must become a way of managing, not an episode that occurs once a year. The purpose is to concentrate effort, time, and resources on matters that are critically important to the enterprise and to slough off activities that are unnecessary or only marginally significant. This has to be done in operational terms, day by day, every day. Planning must be tied in intimately with running the business. Planning should create a reflexive "why?" at every decision-making occasion. Why are we doing this? Why should we do that? Does it move us in the direction we want to go? What can we do to move in that direction faster—today? The planning process and the planning documentation must be conceived and designed so as to be a working tool to guide daily operating decisions to maximize the major thrusts of the enterprise.

The best place to start encouraging that "why?" reflex is right in the CEO's office. Every time a suggestion, proposal, or request is submitted, the first questions should be: Why should we do it? What are we going to get out of it? Do we need it? Does it contribute to our major strategic thrust? If these questions cannot be answered specifically and convincingly, refuse to consider the matter further. Send it back to the drawing board. The word will get around.

Insist that action plans be completed, particularly at the lowest levels of responsibility, and then insist that all your managers monitor their control points regularly. That does not mean constantly looking over their subordinates' shoulders. Remember, those control points are measures of results, not actions. If the results are forthcoming, you can tolerate great flexibility in action.

But if you or your colleagues are going to monitor results, you have to be able to see the results. It is ironic how many planning teams will lay out a well-thought-through and logically structured set of objectives only to conclude that their accounting system does not produce data in terms of the objectives. They have set sales objectives for strategic business units, but the order processing section does not break out sales that way. They have profitability objectives by SBU, but no way to identify working capital requirements by SBU. Who is running the company? By setting objectives in the terms you did, you have decided that these are the critical dimensions of progress for the company. Change the management information system so that it does provide the information you have decided is critical. While you are at it, you may find you can eliminate a lot of accounting data that you are not going to do anything about anyway.

And then there is compensation. It is amazing how many managers are reluctant to talk about compensation. But in any culture, the forms of recognition define the values of the society. In a business environment, the various forms of compensation provide the overt expression of what is considered important. Put bluntly: If you want planned results, pay for them. If your reward structure is not closely related to the achievement of planned objectives, you are kidding yourself if you think you are pursuing purposeful strategies—kidding *yourself*, not the rest of the organization. They get the message loud and clear.

Delegation

The little arithmetic lesson in the earlier chapter is not universally appreciated. Let's walk through it again from a CEO's point of view. You have key result objectives in sales, earnings, and profitability—and in the development area, one in market penetration and one in diversification. Five in all. You have segmented the business into six strategic business units, each of which has sales, earnings, and profitability objectives. Six times 3 is 18 control points. Three specific markeis are targeted for penetration and a product development and an acquisition objective for diversification. Three plus 2 plus 18 gives 23 control points—perfectly manageable.

But you have six SBU marketing plans with at least five action programs each. Your earnings plan will have cost-savings programs, productivity objectives, integration plans—whatever—that will number a dozen or more. Your profitability/financial plan may have a like number. Your market penetration, diversification, and acquisition subobjectives will have several action plans each. Then, remember there are action plans to correct weaknesses. By most conservative calculations, there are more than 60 action plans. Over a period of a couple of months, you can spend an hour apiece with the responsible managers going over each of these plans. But to bring them all before a planning committee? That is a week and a half of solid meetings. With a ten-person planning committee, do you know what that would cost? And if the planning committee tried to participate in the development of those action plans? It won't fly.

You are a captive of the arithmetic. If you are going to do effective planning, you must delegate some of the detailed planning activities down into the organization. That is where the participation comes in. To do that, though, you have to trust your people and your management structure. That may require some training in planning techniques, but the very best training device is to make it abundantly clear that you will hold people fully accountable for the objective results they have agreed to. That will get their attention at least. The second necessary technique is to refuse to consider any half-baked plans. Insist that people do their homework, get the necessary information, consult with appropriate colleagues, and think through what is realistically possible. Do not let them "delegate up" their planning responsibility to the planning committee.

We used the CEO as an example, but all senior executives have the same problem. The sales/marketing vice-president is responsible for six SBU sales objectives. Assume this person has four sales regions and a national accounts manager; already he or she has 20–25 control points. The vice-president cannot reasonably expect to be the major architect of the specific action programs that will be pursued in each of those regions to reach the sales objectives. He or she must depend on the regional sales managers to present completed action plan proposals for review, suggestions, and approval.

Managements just beginning to undertake planning almost invariably get overinvolved in the details of implementing the plans. Too much significant but not essential information is brought before the planning committee. Worst of all, presented with all this unorganized information, the planning committee succumbs to the temptation to design the action plans around the conference table. A committee is a terrible place to design anything. (You have probably heard the quip about a camel being a horse designed by committee.) No matter how much information is available, there is never enough. Furthermore, there is neither time nor opportunity for the mental synthesis process to occur. A ten-person committee, no matter how competent, working on a design problem for an hour will never accomplish as much as one of their number working on it for a whole day. Attempting to work out action plans in a planning committee is responsible more than anything else for the complaint that planning takes too much time. It takes a completely impossible amount of time if everybody tries to do everything.

The problem is most pervasive in relatively small and

young companies where at least some of the managers hark back to the recent past when in fact everybody did on occasion do everything and was involved in all the major decisions of the enterprise. There is a natural nostalgia for those exciting times and a professed reluctance to become too "formal" and "dehumanized." If you flip that coin over, though, you may find that the other side says something about lack of mutual respect and confidence among the management peers. Those reservations must be addressed directly and laid to rest. The quickest way to do that is to assign clearly stated result responsibility to individuals and make it explicit that they will be held fully accountable for performance. You can call that putting a person on the spot. You can also read it as an expression of confidence in the competence of the individual.

The hyperinvolvement syndrome persists sometimes in more sophisticated managements that subscribe to a collegial or participative concept of management. These are powerful concepts, but they must not be interpreted to imply an ongoing debating society. Participation must be provided for in a very careful structure for it to work. Otherwise, it becomes "anybody's business is everybody's business," which just will not get the job done.

One final word about planning committees: It is quite common for a CEO when convening such a committee to say something to the effect that the group is to act as a collective chief executive concerned with the overall health of the enterprise. That is quite fitting and proper. In the complex contemporary business world, team planning of strategy has proven to be very effective if not essential. The alternative is for the planning committee to act in an advisory capacity to the CEO, who retains the personal responsibility for making all the strategic decisions. This seems to work for some people.

But a planning team can function only to supply collective judgment to arrive at critical strategic decisions. Yes, a committee properly operated can make decisions. What it cannot do is implement those decisions. As far as a strategic plan is concerned, seeing that the plan works remains the responsibility of the CEO. That cannot be delegated. Reserve the very expensive time of the committee for those things it can really do—namely, apply its collective experience, specialized knowledge, judgment, and maybe even gut feeling to deciding where the company should go and what the best way is to get there.

Organization

Probably the most mischievous cliche in management is that "authority must be commensurate with responsibility." It compellingly invites the excuse, "I did not get the job done because I was not given adequate authority." Nobody has adequate authority to get the job done. The president of the United States doesn't. Certainly, a corporate CEO does not.

Things get done through negotiating, co-opting, logrolling, wheedling, perhaps threatening, but seldom through direct orders. Authoritarian management may have worked in the nineteenth century, but with every passing year, it becomes less practicable in a society that resists arbitrary direction.

However, organizational structure can expedite the negotiating process or make it needlessly complex. If in setting your planning objectives, you find one name on the majority of the "responsibility" lines, or if you have difficulty deciding just who should be responsible and are tempted to split the responsibility or appoint a steering committee, it suggests that your organizational structure is not congruent with the pattern of work to be done. This in itself will not make it impossible to control your planned progress or achieve your objectives, but it increases the odds against you. If you succumb to the temptation to assign dual responsibility, it increases the negative odds even more. At the very least, awkward organizational relationships consume a lot of management time and make life difficult for everyone. Why not rearrange the organization so that it follows the work flow?

When you get your plan done, let it talk to you a little bit. Are the responsibilities for producing results reasonably distributed among the talent available? Is too much direct responsibility flowing to the top when it could be parcelled out to lower levels? Do you really need product managers in order to manage strategies effectively? Should manufacturing really be responsible for its own quality control? Is the interaction between research and engineering too tenuous? Should you consider development task forces? Is there no logical place to locate responsibility for development objectives except at a junior level? Is that the way you want it?

And most important: Is there no obvious person responsible for earnings performance except the CEO, other than possibly the financial officer? This is frequently the case, and it is a severe organizational weakness. The CEO needs some backup in this function. Otherwise, he or she will either overconcentrate on it and neglect the long-term needs of the enterprise, or give earnings inadequate attention, with ultimately disastrous consequences. The financial officer is seldom a good viceroy in this matter. The financial officer is usually not intimately enough familiar with the operations, and often his or her only medium for influencing earnings is the budget, which is a very blunt instrument indeed. The best leveraged position to exercise this control is the production officer. Earnings are the difference between price and cost. In large measure, the market will determine price. What management has most control over is cost, and the production person is in the best position to affect costs. There is good evidence that American industry has lost sight of this fact. The production people have been pushed out of or withdrawn from the strategic planning process. The consequence has been slackened productivity, inappropriate manufacturing facilities (either too much or too little), and ultimate loss of competitiveness. You may have to reeducate your production person somewhat if you are to assign him or her this responsibility, but the results may be well worth it.

The organizational implications of planning may be considered a by-product benefit. Certainly, the dictum "form follows function," although formulated in a different context, should apply with full force to corporate organization. The structure of what you have decided is important to accomplish is undoubtedly the best possible guide to how your personnel resources should be deployed. However, as with so much of the planning process, the relationship is iterative. If you let your plans lead you to modifying organizational relationships, you increase the likelihood that your plans will be realized.

Credibility

The worst affliction any strategic plan can have is a lack of credibility. If people think it is a lot of blue sky, a lot of wishful thinking, they will resent the time they spend on preparing it and privately snicker at the management that propounds it. Chances are that one of your early plans turned out to be an absolute pipe dream, and now you have to deal with this problem. There are two rather straightforward therapies, one attitudinal and one procedural. Applied consistently and conscientiously, they will almost always work.

The first is to establish a culture of accountability. People must be convinced that when their name goes down on an objective they are fully expected to achieve it. If you have not established that attitude yet, you will have to sit down with people and tell them the ground rules are changed. Some people are going to buck and scream over making such a commitment. Negotiate them down: "What level of results would you be willing to commit to?" Some people will anticipate you and discount their proposed objectives to levels that they are sure they can reach without risk. Try to expose them if you can; but if they are insistent, take their word for it. This violates the common principle that objectives should have some stretch in them, should encourage people to extend themselves. But given a choice, it is better to accept modest objectives and achieve them than to set heroic ones that no one believes are likely to be attained. It gives credibility to the process and reassures the responsible manager. After a cycle or two, when the panic reaction subsides, you may be able to elicit some more ambitious objectives. For the present, you will have to be content to add up the planned performance and comment, "This is not really a very impressive plan. We should be able to do better than this."

The other way to squeeze the water out of plans is to take

advantage of the multidimensional and the iterative nature of the process. When you take your first cut at setting objectives and subobjectives, check the following:

1. Is there anything in your policy structure that would work against the objective?
2. Have you identified a strategic weakness that will have to be eliminated before you can realistically expect to achieve the objective?
3. Is the objective bucking a trend in the environment? What makes you think you can make water flow uphill? Particularly, is the objective compatible with your assessment of the competitive environment? If you are planning to expand sales faster than the market is growing, whom are you going to take market share away from? How?
4. Are you proposing a price policy that is contrary to the trend in the market? Why will people pay your higher price?
5. If you are proposing a new product introduction, how will it differ from products already available? Who cares? Is that segment of the market big enough or growing fast enough to justify the sales objective?
6. If you are anticipating a cost reduction, do you know of anyone in the industry who is achieving that kind of performance?
7. If you are planning a new product development, is anyone in the industry already working along parallel lines and likely to get there before you?

If the objectives can pass this kind of qualitative screen, you do not need to be too concerned about their quantitative validity *if* you know they are going to be rubbed against reality at lower echelons of the organization. The planning committee does not have to see clearly exactly how the objectives are going to be accomplished if somebody somewhere in the hierarchy does know and will commit himself or herself to the accomplishment. If, however, when the plan is cascaded down through the levels of the organization the people in the trenches who will ultimately have to make it happen cannot see any way to do it, you want that information to feed back up and disabuse you of your comfortable illusions. The gathering and analysis of information, the checking of assumptions, and the summation of individual commitments should be done down there close to where the action is. Then, if the hierarchy of objectives is added back up to the key result objectives and the sums confirm their reasonableness, you have some assurance that they are in fact attainable.

But you must allow time for this iteration. You must involve a lot of people in the planning process, which probably means that someone will have to provide appropriate coaching and, perhaps, formal training to some additional people. But if you do it right, you will have an objective structure that has stood the test of intimate knowledge and enjoys widespread commitment. That is your best guarantee that the plans will work out.

Incompetence

The Peter Principle notwithstanding, sheer incompetence is not a major cause of plans going awry. It does happen, though, even with chief executive officers. Let's be honest about it. When incompetence does happen it provides an opportunity for one of the substantial benefits of planned management. There is some justification for the common apprehension among managers faced with the prospect of the introduction of planning into their organization. A glib tongue, long experience, or obscure records will no longer substitute for actual performance in the presence of clearly stated objectives and strict accountability for results. The vast majority of managers will rise to the challenge and eventually gain greater confidence in their abilities through the greater effectiveness of focused effort. A few, however, will be shaken out. What can we say? Planning did not create the incompetence. It merely exposed it. Certainly, the organization is better off facing up to the ineluctable necessity to make some reassignment of responsibility. Sometimes a reassignment proves beneficial to both the individual and the organization. If a separation is unavoidable, it can only be hoped that the person involved will be more comfortable in a less stressful situation where performance is less demanding.

Planning Directors

Should you have a full-time planning director? Obviously, it depends in large measure on your size and resources. Also it depends on what you want him or her to do. Certainly, there must be one individual who coordinates the mechanics of planning, keeps the planning calendar, needles people when necessary, and supervises the documentation of the plan. This can be the president, a staff vice-president, or even a line vice-president if someone has the inclination and the technique to divert enough of his or her time to engage in this activity. I have even seen a general counsel take on this assignment and become so intrigued that he eventually dropped almost all his legalistic responsibilities. It will take time, though. It will not be accomplished incidentally, as you may have already discovered. If there is no one who is really anxious for this assignment or if your original assignee has lost his or her enthusiasm, you had better think about assigning someone full time to the task. You are devoting a lot of expensive management time to the process already, and it may be false economy to have the effort dribbled away for lack of coordination.

You have several options in choosing a planning director. You can appoint a fairly junior person who will function as a little bit of a high-grade "gofer"—arranging meetings, shuffling papers, reminding people of deadlines, preparing documents, and so on. This has the advantage, first of all, of being cheap. It also does not pose a threat to any of the senior executives, which can be an important consideration. The corollary of that, of course, is that this person must have the backing of the CEO or he or she will get terribly frustrated trying to get people's attention. It is a good job for a bright young comer, because it will provide wide exposure to all the affairs of the company.

The second option is to assign some old-timer with an analytical turn of mind who perhaps would like to step back from line responsibilities for a few years. This option can be very successful if you have the right person. He or she will bring a lot of knowledge of the industry and of the internal operations of the company. But this person will also bring along a lot of baggage of interpersonal relations and biases accumulated over a long career. This can present problems. You do not want an abrasive personality or a congenitally frustrated person in this job.

Another option is to hire a professional. Good ones are expensive, and it would be strictly fortuitous if you could get one who is familiar with your industry. Lack of familiarity is not as much of a problem as you might think, because a good planning professional will come up to speed remarkably fast. His or her biggest problem will be to pick up the jargon and establish credibility with your executives. If you expect to need a lot of staff work from the planning office—analysis, evaluations, critiques of appropriations requests, and so on— you may be well advised to bring in an expert. His or her knowledge of information sources and special services, network of personal contacts, and technical expertise may make this the most cost-effective course in the long run.

The final possibility applies only in special situations. It is becoming increasingly common for the planning director's spot to be a staging area for the next CEO. From the outside, it is not always possible to tell whether this happens by conscious intent or consequentially. In a sense it does not matter. Was the nominee put in that position to have a couple of years to plot out the long-range future of the enterprise that he or she was expected to administer, or was this person a sharp strategist who ultimately moved in on the president and took over? Either case demonstrates the pivotal position of the planning office for gaining a grasp on the really important strategic dimensions of a company.

Except in the case of the "president-in-waiting," you want to be sure that actual planning is not abdicated by top management in favor of the planning director. A good planning director can do many things:

- Provide rigorous and objective analysis of a variety of situations.
- Come up with innovative ideas and strategic options that might not occur to executives closer to the operations.
- Act as a communicator and trainer to propagate the planning process down the organization.
- Be the conscience of the organization to see that the officers keep their eyes on the main chance and do not get distracted by seductive but irrelevant possibilities.

What the planning director should not do is try to plan for the organization. That must be done by the people with the power of decision and the responsibility for action. If the planning office starts to plan, you will open up a chasm between that office and operations that may be impossible to bridge.

There is one other inherent problem you should be sensitive to. To the extent that the planning director works for and with the corporate planning committee or the president's office and at the same time coaches divisional or SBU management on the formulation of their plans, he or she is put in a very ambiguous position. In the one role, the planning director is helping the subunit to put together the most convincing proposal possible. Then subsequently, he or she may be expected to act as top management's "chief prosecutor" in critiquing that proposal. There is no way these two roles can be fully resolved, although it does help to clarify them as much as possible. Basically it comes down to who needs help the most. If top managers have become relatively sophisticated about planning, they should be able to evaluate a plan on their own and the planning director can be both a player–coach and cheerleader for the subunit. If this is not the case, then the planning director must hold back with the subunit and be an advisor on format, sources of information, rigor of analysis, but not a participant in the planning decisions. Even so, if a subunit's plan is rejected, its leaders may still feel betrayed by the planner. This, unfortunately, may be unavoidable.

In either case, it is not a bad idea for the planner to act as the devil's advocate at a dress rehearsal of the plan presentation. There should be a little adversarial flavor in any such presentation, and a little practice in sounding like you know what you are talking about cannot hurt.

L'envoi

So how do you make your plans come to pass? You do it and do it and do it until you get it right. And you keep track of what you are doing and of the consequences of what you have done. You make sure that you are getting regular feedback on progress in the directions that you have decided are important. Planning will not keep you from making mistakes, but if you build in proper feedback, it will let you make a lot of little mistakes but no big ones. And when you start to do something stupid, you will find out early enough to stop it quickly and try something else. Keep your feedback in terms of results, in terms of your declared objectives. It's not really important whether the actions are carried out just the way they were planned if the results are forthcoming. In fact, just the opposite. You want the actions to be adjusted just as far down the hierarchy as possible so that the adjustments can be made quickly and with the maximum amount of pertinent information. What you want is constancy of purpose, but flexibility of action.

For Additional Information

Kastens, M. L., "Whatever Happened to Plant Managers?" *Management Today* (August 1973).

Documents and comments on the loss of influence of production executives in top management decisions. Of historical interest because the article was rejected by all major U.S. management journals because of "lack of interest in the subject." Ultimately, it was published in the United Kingdom. Now it is a hot subject.

Koontz, H., and O'Donnell, C., *Management: A Systems and Contingency Analysis of Managerial Functions.* New York: McGraw-Hill Book Company, 1976. Part 6, pp. 639–740.

One of the chief gurus of control theory points out that effective controls require plans. Also goes into some detail to show how to assure that your management information system really provides control information, not just a lot of electronic noise.

13
Gaudeamus Igitur— Therefore Let Us Rejoice

Planning is a learning experience. Learning planning techniques is not important. What is important is learning how your industry functions, how your company operates, how your market reacts. Try to remember back five years ago, before you tried formal planning. How did you ever manage with so little information about your markets, your competition, the dynamics of your own cost structure? Inconceivable!

Maybe by now you have your planning process run in and are smoothly making subtle adjustments from year to year. Maybe you still feel a little awkward. You don't feel you yet have the knack of it. In either case, you are still learning, and the more you plan, the more you will learn. It may not always be apparent, but if you have struggled with strategic plans for five years, you have come a long way.

In *Long-Range Planning for Your Business*, I promised you that once you tried planning you would like it. I am afraid that was a little hyperbolic. It is not all beer and skittles. In fact, it gets pretty sweaty at times. One reason is that some of the things you learn you would rather not know. Still, though being a passenger on a roller coaster may be more exciting, for the long haul it is more comfortable to be driving your own car and taking it where you want to go.

There have been some pretty rough times since 1976. Some managements were forced to abandon the wheelhouse while everybody manned the pumps. Survival became *the* objective. Others, perhaps those with a little more momentum or maybe just better nerves, were able to pare their plans down, stretch them out, but still stay on course although at reduced speed. That is what good planning should enable you to do. It will not help you predict, much less prevent, a major recession, but it should make it possible to react quickly and effectively to the slings and arrows when they come. It guides you to constructive response, because you have learned the dynamics of the business and you know where the critical pressure points are. You know what to hold and what to fold.

Figure 10.   Interquartile range of return on equity distribution.

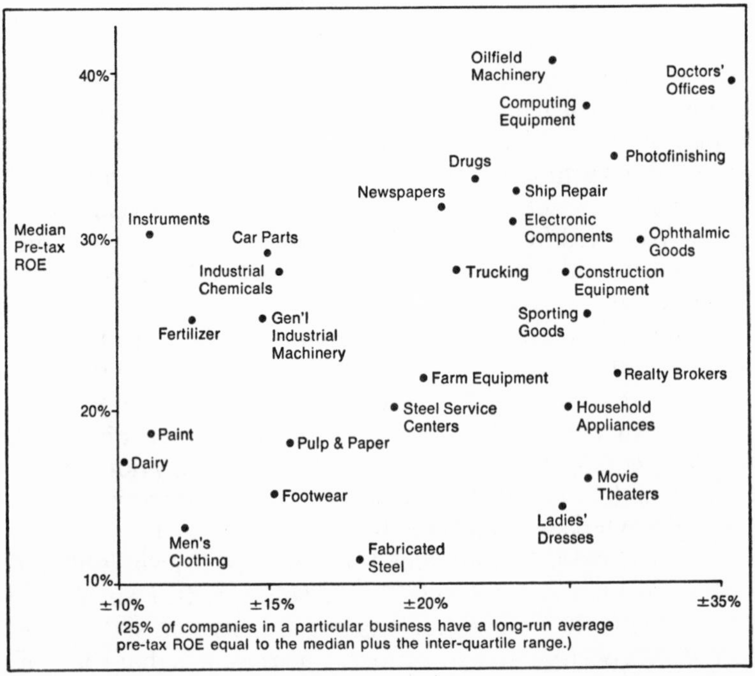

You can stretch out a plan if you have one. If you do not have one and must improvise one after the stuff hits the fan, you may end up taking a bath.

The other instructive observation during the period between the mid-1970s and early 1980s was that, while some companies were stumbling toward Chapter 11, others, apparently in the same industry, were proceeding with barely perceptible slackening of their previous progress. You could find examples in almost every industry. I do not have the data to support the contention that the planned managements came through relatively unscathed and the hip-shooters foundered. But one thing is clear: Management does matter! Strategic planning may be the technique of putting a company in the right place at the right time, but management has to *do* something when it gets there.

All the talk in recent years about the importance of strategic positioning and "doing the right things rather than doing things right" has obscured the essential fact that there are good operators and bad operators. It is hard to fault the massive statistical evidence that PIMS has assembled to correlate various statistical parameters with profitability of companies, but within those statistically significant correlations, there can be a wide range of deviations. Figure 10 records one of the few attempts to document that range.

Good strategies make it easier to be successful, but they do not guarantee success. People have to make it happen. Good people are always in short supply at any level in any organization. If you could have an ideal incumbent in every job slot, running a company would be a breeze. But you won't. What planning can do is assure that the always imperfect talent is directed to significant tasks. Even a dull tool will make an impression if it is skillfully handled.

But to get that benefit, you must finish the planning task. It is not sufficient to position the enterprise optimally and to set the targets skillfully. You must pursue the system through to where the action will occur and ensure that the direction is clear and the performance is feasible.

Action. Change. Accountability. But the first requirement is action. Without this, the rest is "sounding brass, or a tinkling cymbal."

Index

174

DATE DUE
